BUILDING IN A BROKEN WORLD

Building in a Broken World

BROTHER ANDREW

KINGSWAY PUBLICATIONS

EASTBOURNE

ISBN 0 86065 170 3

Printed in Great Britain for
KINGSWAY PUBLICATIONS LTD
Lottbridge Drove, Eastbourne, E. Sussex BN23 6NT by
Richard Clay (The Chaucer Press) Ltd, Bungay, Suffolk

I would like to thank
Dale Kietzman
and Dan Wooding
for their invaluable editorial help
in the preparation of this book,
as well as my secretaries
who typed and retyped the script.

CONTENTS

INTRODUCTION

What a wonderful time for building! We live in a world that is hopelessly confused, torn, sinful. That's precisely when we can expect God to step in with a fresh outpouring of grace and love.

How will he do it? Through men and women like you and me. Why was the Bible written? To show us how fully the grace of God can be displayed in the lives of ordinary men and women. Every biographical sketch in the Bible teaches us that God can do exactly the same thing through you and me.

I've selected the life of Nehemiah for two reasons. First, Nehemiah identified with people in their need. That, of course, made life risky for him; it made him a pioneer. That gave him the opportunity to pay the price: hardship, opposition, loneliness, weariness— the price everyone who is in a position of spiritual leadership has to pay.

Second, the Book of Nehemiah, like so many other books in the Bible, is like a miniature Bible. I think I can say that about almost every book in the Bible. That is what makes Bible study so fascinating. Every single book presents some aspect of the kingdom of God and teaches us how we can advance his kingdom. Every book tells us about the problems created by people. Every book then shows us that God chooses a man to be a mediator, or that God appoints a man to restore the nation. We see that same pattern in Nehemiah.

In this one little book God's plan is stated: sin interferes with God's purposes; God finds a way of deliverance and redemption; that way is worked through one dedicated person who changes the whole situation again to the favor of God. That, in fact, is a short summary not only of the Book of Nehemiah but of every book in the Bible, and of God's dealing in the lives of countless thousands of his humblest servants.

In Nehemiah, Jerusalem is rebuilt. It all started with one man who got the vision. He got the vision because he was honest enough to ask questions. Because he had the vision, he was also given the responsibility for the task. And the vision and the task combined in one man to make him a leader.

Do you want to be a leader? There are many lessons to be learned. The life of Nehemiah is an excellent place to start learning. God has recorded Nehemiah's life so that you can identify with it. God is saying you can do what Nehemiah did.

Of course, I am not going to deal with every detail of the Book of Nehemiah. I am only going to point out the incidents in his life that will help in the development of our own personalities and ministries, and that will give us the opportunity to study the ways of God with man. And that will help us in our outreach to the world.

PART ONE

ONE
BUILDING
IN A BROKEN
UGANDA

It was on April 12, 1978, that Idi Amin's soldiers invaded the Makerere Gospel Mission to Uganda church in the Kampala suburb of Makerere. The crazed gunmen sprayed bullets at the platform. The gunfire then screamed skyward and riddled holes in the asbestos roof.

As the mayhem continued, many of the six-hundred-strong congregation quickly dropped to their knees between the pews, and with arms upraised they began to praise God. The well-built brick building that I knew so well from my visit to the country in 1977 was filled with a cacophony of incredible sound—a mixture of prayer, praise, and bullets.

Some two hundred members of the congregation were arrested, beaten, and then hauled off to the infamous Nakasero State Research Bureau headquarters where thousands of Ugandans had already been put to death by Amin's terror machine.

These courageous believers—my friends—sat huddled in a circle with guns pressed against their necks. Gasoline cans were put around them, and they were told they were to be burned alive. The fiery end was to come as soon as the execution orders arrived from General Mustafa Adrisi, Idi Amin's second-in-command.

This brave band of people prayed silently. As they did, something incredible happened. The car carrying Adrisi and his aides was involved in a terrible car crash. The "accident" took place on the main Kampala-Jinja road, and Adrisi was badly injured. The crash spared my friends' lives but did not prevent them from suffering months of terrible torture for their faith.

In the July of the following year—after Amin had been deposed by the invading Tanzanian army—those prisoners were among the cast of an unusual dramatic presentation at the church which still bore the marks on its walls and roof of that brutal attack.

It was standing room only as the curtains made from blankets were opened on a makeshift stage, and many of those who once were nearly burned alive performed to a packed church. The play began with one of the ex-prisoners reading out Idi Amin's fateful speech in September, 1977, banning twenty-seven denominations, including theirs. Without mocking the ex-president, this man read Amin's allegations that the group was part of the CIA, and added "Big Daddy's" instructions to the soldiers to "beat and kill anybody found worshiping."

What was the subject of the drama that drew such a crowd in post-Amin Uganda? It was the story of Nehemiah going to rebuild the broken wall around Jerusalem. The Old Testament story had obvious significance for the churches of Uganda, which had seen hundreds of thousands of their brothers and sisters murdered by Amin and his henchmen.

Written by a talented church member, the play leaped from those Old Testament days to a clever scene in Amin's Uganda. For instance, the actors portrayed Nehemiah's party of workers going through a border post manned by Amin's guards. The congregation applauded wildly as it saw the border officer dressed, and acting, like a State Research officer. He was wearing dark glasses, platform heels, and bell-bottom trousers.

This officer had, until "Nehemiah" arrived, been confiscating all valuables from those who passed through his hands, and then many were sent for further mistreatment and possible death.

When I heard about this play, I realized how relevant the story of Nehemiah is to us all today. It's as important now in

Uganda today as it is in the rest of this broken world of hatred and war.

One reason why this story is so relevant is that Nehemiah was a man who asked honest questions. In chapter 1, verse 2, he recalls "that Hanani, one of my brethren, came with certain men out of Judah; and I asked them concerning the Jews that survived, who had escaped exile, and concerning Jerusalem" (RSV).

Nehemiah was living far away from his own country. That was not his fault. Some generations before, his nation had turned away from God. God's protection had then been taken away from them, and the enemy came in and took the young people captive into another country.

Nehemiah's parents were among those people sent into exile. So I could say that Nehemiah was living in the wrong place—but that was not his fault.

Many of us may feel we are living in the wrong place, but it is generally not our personal responsibility, because things which happened in the lives of our parents or grandparents, or in the history of our church or our nation, are not our responsibility. So do not accept any accusation from the devil that, because circumstances are all wrong, it's your fault.

But I also want you to be honest enough to face your situation as it is today, not thinking that you have to place blame on someone, but with the attitude that says, "Lord, if I can do anything about it, I am willing."

In Nehemiah, we see a man living in exile, making the best he can of a situation—a thing which every one of us would naturally do. Then a few of his friends happen to pay him a visit. He asks them a question. Right here is where the secret of his success begins.

People in our churches today sometimes complain that preachers answer questions no one is asking. That's terrible! But there is one thing far more terrible—that's when no one is asking any questions.

Are we asking questions?

When I meet a person, I say, "How do you do?" Wait a minute! Who gives me the right to ask, "How do you do?" What am I after? Suppose that a person has a big need. Just because I asked, is that person going to unburden his or her heart? Am

I really interested in the other person's problems?

Let me tell you the truth. When we ask, "How do you do?" we don't really expect an answer. We really couldn't care less! Do you think I want to know all your problems? It's simply natural for me to ask you how you are getting on. But I'm not really interested in your problems. I don't have the resources to solve your problems, and I don't have time to listen to all of them anyhow.

Do you realize how hypocritical we can become because we do not mean what we say? Before we ask anyone about his problems, we ought to *earn* the right to do so by showing genuine concern.

I just want to sound a word of warning. We too easily ask about other people's lives without a real willingness to get deeply involved in their problems. Be careful when you ask a question of another person, because most people are at the bursting point with problems.

I admire Nehemiah. He had made the most of the circumstances of his own personal life. Yet he had the courage to make inquiries about the need of his own people in Jerusalem. But once he had asked that question, he could never be the same again!

The courage to ask questions will change your life. I can vouch for that.

My life was certainly transformed in 1955 when I was invited to attend a youth festival in Warsaw, Poland. While there I used every opportunity during this token display of liberty to make contact with Christians. I soon discovered the desperate need for Bibles, teaching aids, encouragement, and love from outside. The Polish believers felt that they had been forgotten.

About 30,000 foreigners had flocked into the country to see, at first hand, what had been described as a "worker's paradise." We were all taken on tours to see the work that the Communists had done to rebuild Warsaw after it had been so devastated by the Nazis. Almost everyone I spoke to was taken in with the idyllic picture of Warsaw that was being presented to gullible tourists.

The group I was staying with all boarded together in a

school building. A Communist sympathizer from Amsterdam told me one day how enthusiastic he was about what he had seen and heard. He couldn't understand why I was not.

"Why don't you skip tomorrow's guided tour, and go on your own," I told Hans. "Go into the main street, turn left, and then you will see some heaps of rubble. Go close to the rubble and when you find an opening, go in and you will find people there. Talk to them and see if they consider this to be a paradise on earth."

Hans looked at me in disbelief and shook his head. Surely he too hadn't been taken in? He was a thinking Dutchman. To his credit, he did go out and inquire for himself. He went into the slum areas on his own, into the ruins where the people lived.

That evening I saw Hans again. He looked pale and frightened. "Andrew, I'm leaving tonight on the midnight train. I am scared stiff by what I have seen and heard today."

I told the "thinking Dutchman" that he had at last seen what I had been taking in since I had arrived. "No one else in about 30,000 visitors to the city has seen what you have today, Hans. You see, they are not prepared to ask questions. They only want to be on the guided tour and see the nice things."

Another example. If you leave JFK airport in New York City and head into the Bronx, it can be a shattering experience. If you talk with people there, you may have to get involved like David Wilkerson did. There are many unsolved needs in the slums of New York, as there are in cities like Amsterdam and London.

Asking questions changes your life. You have to ask questions with a willingness to get involved and lose everything because of what you have seen and heard. That is why Mother Teresa has committed her life to the poor and dying of Calcutta. She asked penetrating questions and then acted to help.

That Polish experience certainly changed the direction of my life. Up until then, I was heading for Indonesia as a missionary.

As a student, I had attended the Glasgow, Scotland, college of the Worldwide Evangelization Crusade. The students had visiting missionaries from all over the world come and lecture about their "field." Later I analyzed this and I asked the faculty, "Have you ever had a missionary here from any Communist country?" I was told that none had ever visited the college.

"Why not?" I asked. The countries under Communist domination then were one-third of the world—now it's half. I therefore had to ask myself: Why is the mission called The *Worldwide* Evangelization Crusade? Their missionaries only cover half of the world. That goes for other societies who also claim their outreach is worldwide. I think they should all consider a name change—or better still, start moving personnel behind the Iron and Bamboo curtains.

TWO
A DREAM-SHATTERING MINISTRY

Many preachers are "six feet beyond contradiction." That means they stand in their lofty pulpits and preach but don't allow their congregations to question their assertions. Why not? Is it a fear that they may not have thought through some of their statements? That they don't really know what they believe?

When I conduct meetings now, I often end with a time of questions from the floor. I want the people to "test" what I have said, and if there are things they cannot understand or even agree with, they can put them to me.

Then I ask a question. I challenge them to tell me one country in the world that they, as believers, cannot enter with the gospel. You see, I don't believe there are any closed doors. Hence the name of our mission, Open Doors. I am always happy to share this how-to-get-in information, but I then add, "I can tell you how to get in; but I may not be able to tell you how to get out again." After all, Jesus said in the Great Commission, "Go ye therefore into all the world . . ." He didn't say, "And come back again"!

Christians need constantly to ask questions. It was people's failure to ask honest questions that made Hitler successful. Already in 1936 the concentration camps were full, yet except for men like Niemoeller and Bonhoeffer, nobody inside Germany dared ask what really was happening in the country at that time. If they had, and then acted, we would have a totally different world now, and the Church would have a totally different involvement. Then we would see that our money is not to be spent on structures, on "Plushy Cathedrals," but on followers of Jesus, free or persecuted, which is the real Church. We deprive ourselves of the privilege by not asking ourselves pertinent questions. We go to foreign countries as businessmen and tourists and then do not ask deep, penetrating questions about what really is happening to our brothers and sisters.

I believe that Open Doors should have a dream-shattering ministry to sleeping Christians. While in Guatemala in Central America early in 1980, I came to realize that many of the Christians there simply didn't want to know about the persecution of believers in a section of their country. We had discovered that in the Queche Province, all the missionaries had either been expelled, threatened, or had run off, and so the churches were left alone. However church leaders in the capital, Guatemala City, still said that there was nothing wrong. Everything was fine.

We persisted and our personnel raised this matter at a conference there. Slowly, at first, the delegates began to talk about what had happened and began to ask searching questions. Eventually there was a resolution at the end of the conference that every congregation in Guatemala City should send someone to Queche. They would visit the believers there, whatever their denominations, and ask them how they were, help them in whatever way they could, and tell them they were praying for them.

My friend and colleague, Brother David, who heads up our work into China and has written his moving story in the book *God's Smuggler to China*, is loved by the believers behind the Great Wall for one reason. His first question when he got there was, "How is the Body of Christ?" He didn't ask, "How do you live?" or "Do you get enough food to eat?" but "How is the Body of Christ?" What a question! That's what made him acceptable to the secret church in China.

The word "Nehemiah" means "Comforter given by Jehovah." It is only when we ask the right questions that we can truly be comforters to the suffering Church. But we must first know the need. When you inquire about a certain need, you may ultimately find yourself called to meet that need! And your responsibility is as big as the call.

What is a call? A call is to know about a need. We should obey the Scriptures where Jesus himself, in John 4:35, instructed us to lift up our eyes unto the fields. In other words, get acquainted with the vastness of the need.

Too many Christians say, "I have no call." They say, "God never called me." But I say that you have never heard the call, because God *has* called you. He has told you to get acquainted with the need in the world. We complain sometimes about the modern news media, newspapers and television, that throw all the needs of the world into our living room. Actually, they leave us without a single excuse for saying that we do not know about the need.

It is my earnest conviction that God has given to his children *all the resources* to meet the needs of the world.

God has placed me in the Open Doors ministry, which operates in countries that other people consider to be closed. For many years I have traveled behind the Iron and Bamboo Curtains, asking about my brethren. I have sometimes been terribly lonely because in Western Europe very few Christians were interested in their brethren. That is why nothing happens! That is why the revolution is spreading! And that's why our Western culture is crumbling.

My question is always, "Do you really want to know?" Because if you want to know, you *can* know. And if you want to change the world, you *can* change the world. If you want to build, you *can* build. But first, do you want to know the truth?

When Nehemiah put his question to his brethren, he got a shattering report. Verse 3 says: "The survivors. . .are in great trouble and shame; the wall of Jerusalem is broken down, and its gates are destroyed by fire."

What a terrible picture they painted! But they had clearly stated the need.

We could give the same picture about the world situation today. There is great trouble everywhere. I have wept over the situation in Indochina. I spent much time in Vietnam over a period of ten years. I ministered in the hospitals, and I have never seen so many badly wounded people in my life.

I remember one particularly harrowing visit to a hospital ship that moved along the coast of the war-torn land receiving the broken bodies and minds of wounded American servicemen. I stood on the deck of this floating hospital with my old friend Corrie ten Boom and watched helicopters arriving about every three minutes to discharge their pathetic cargo. It was so disturbing that Corrie eventually had to leave. And Corrie had been incarcerated in a German concentration camp during World War II!

I stayed on because I had been asked to preach to the men. As I stood at the front of a room provided for the meeting on the ship, clasping my Bible, I was horrified to see my congregation being wheeled in. Most of the men were minus arms, legs, eyes. I had been in a military hospital in Indonesia myself, but I had never seen anything like this before. If anyone needed the message of Christ's healing, these men did.

During one visit, I participated in the ordination of Vietnamese pastors; today they are dead! I dedicated church buildings; today they are destroyed!

There is great trouble everywhere: Africa, Asia, the Middle East. Walls are broken down and lie in crumbled heaps. Gates are destroyed.

Let's look again at Nehemiah. His friends had just come from Judah. I don't know what they looked like. They had made a long journey, coming from a very poor area. Nehemiah was probably beautifully dressed because his job was in the palace of the king. So there was obviously quite a difference in outward appearances between the disheveled group from Judah and sophisticated Nehemiah. He had every reason to say, "Why don't you go and get cleaned up, and get yourself a good suit first. I feel a bit embarrassed because you look so ragged."

You know, much of the help we offer people in the poorer countries of the world is on that level. We give bread to hungry people. We give clothing to poor people. And that is *all* the help we give them. And we are very proud that we give so much. We never seem to realize that we have only temporarily eased a symptom, without once treating their real problems. When Nehemiah asked about his own people and about

Jerusalem, he expected an answer, and I know that in his heart he was willing to react to whatever the answer might be. In other words, he was willing to share their problems, to sit down, to listen and pray and help.

This is the moral obligation you have before you dare ask how anybody is. If your attitude is not the same as Nehemiah's, then God is not going to use you.

A word of warning: the moment you know about the need, you have a responsibility. It's just like when two people meet, and one says, "Oh, I have terrible problems." You ask, "Well, what are they?" And the other then shares his problems with you. His problems now become your responsibility. There is just no other way around that. If you dare not accept more responsibility, then you should not ask about his problems. Just live for yourself. That's the choice you have.

We have not been taught to be open to other people's problems. That's why I want to learn from Nehemiah, because I have a personal need here. So often I think that I have enough problems; I don't want to have any more from other people. I know that many times I have surrendered all to the Lord Jesus, but also on other occasions I have said, "Lord, it's too much. I know bearing burdens should be blessing me, but they give me sleepless nights, and I cry when I pray for so many people—it's too many problems. I wish I could be just a little more on my own, and have a few less problems, because then I could enjoy life a little more."

I want to be honest with you. I've often had that reaction. Then I go back to the Word of God, and God speaks to me. I rebel, but God forgives me. Jesus had no problems before he came into the world, but he voluntarily took upon himself all the problems of the whole world. Because he came and took the responsibility for my problems, I am a Christian. And Jesus said, "Follow me," so that has to be my life.

Early on in my Eastern European ministry, I felt the great need for a Russian pocket Bible. But Corry, my wife, and I just didn't have the money to pay for the printing, a total of about $15,000. My total savings toward this project was less than $2,000. So what should I do?

It was then 1963 and I sat down with Corry, who was

expecting a baby, and discussed the value of our house. We loved that place, yet its sale seemed to be the only way I could raise the necessary cash for the pocket Bibles.

Corry's face went white when I first brought up the possibility. "Maybe God doesn't want us to have those pocket Bibles," she said. "Maybe the very slowness of the money coming in is guidance."

Despite this, Corry began to pray that she would think of the house not as our own, but as belonging to God.

"It should be yours to do with as you will," we began praying together every evening. "And yet we know we really don't feel this way, Lord. If you want us to sell the house for the Bibles, you will have to work a small miracle in our hearts to make us willing."

The new baby was born. Cash gifts came in for our child, and we dutifully put it into the Bible fund. But Corry and I knew that even if we continued saving for the next twenty years, at this rate, it would still not be enough. Finally we stopped asking for willingness and just asked God to make us *willing* to be *willing* to let go of the house.

One day the Lord answered our prayer. Corry and I both knew that we really didn't need the house or anything else materially to make us happy as husband and wife.

"I don't know where we'll live," Corry told me. "Remember, Andy? 'We don't know where we're going,' " she said, quoting a saying we had spoken so often.

"But we're going there together," I added.

Immediately we got the house appraised, and the total, along with our savings account, came to just over $15,000. The breakthrough had come. The house was put up for sale and I contacted a printer in England, and asked him to start making the plates we had previously talked about. Corry and I were so happy because we had finally let go of "our" house and made it "his" house.

Amazingly, despite a housing shortage in our village, no one came to view the property. It didn't seem to make sense. Then, one afternoon, a phone call came in from the Bible Society, requesting me to visit their office. Slightly bewildered, I met with their board of directors. I was moved as they said *they* would pay for the entire printing of the pocket Bibles, and all I would need to pay for was my supplies only.

When I returned home, I hugged Corry and told her: "Praise the Lord. We don't have to sell the house." Naturally, she was delighted. The Lord really honored our willingness to sell, for the Russian pocket Bible became an absolute best-seller. And the house? We stayed for another eight years.

Nehemiah asked searching questions of his friends. If God is going to use us, we'll have to have the courage to inquire about the needs of the world, about the needs of our fellow Christians, about the persecution that's in the world today, about the needs of the remote tribes that have not heard the gospel yet, that have no portion of the Scripture in their languages. We have to have enough concern to look at the whole world and say, "How is the gospel going?" As you hear about the need, your honest inquiries will result in a call. And your call will be as big as your enlarged vision of the need.

In the call and preparation of Nehemiah we see the pattern that God wants to follow with us. Here is a man of good standing who has relatives living far away in very difficult circumstances. Somehow God arranges circumstances in such a way that Nehemiah meets people who come from Judah, who could give him vital information.

The only question that remains is: Is this man willing to receive that information? Because if he, or you or I, receive certain kinds of information, then we can never be the same any more.

Just as Nehemiah asked his friends concerning the Jews and Jerusalem, if we want God to use our lives, then we will have to have the courage to make inquiries about the world situation. What is the need in the world? Where is the biggest need? Is it spiritual or physical? What are we going to do about it? Are we going to work on the symptoms, or are we going to work on the causes?

Perhaps I oversimplify by saying the basic problem in the world is sin, but saying that doesn't really help you, because I still have not told you enough to give you a clue as to what you could do about it. If sin is the basic problem in the world, then of course Jesus Christ is the basic solution to the problem. But even saying that does not give you enough specific information to do something about it.

In John 21, the disciples of Jesus faced the same dilemma. Peter said to the other disciples, "I am going out fishing," and the others said, "We will go with you." I think they knew better than anyone else at that time that sin was the problem in the world; and they certainly knew better than anyone else that Jesus was the solution to the problem; and they also knew, somewhere in the back of their minds, that they were to play a tremendous role in spreading the gospel—but they didn't know where to begin. They probably hadn't been fishing for a long time, so the best thing they could think of was, "Let's go fishing."

How many, many Christians today just go back to fishing? Sure, they know that sin is the basic problem; they know that Jesus came to die for the sin of the world. But how can these two basic truths be applied by them in such a way that they will be able to do something about it? That is the biggest problem we face right now.

Let's be realistic. There is no sense in saying that just because I cannot reach some big ideal far away, therefore I will do nothing today. Then I would say with Peter, "I am going out fishing." Well, I am not in that kind of fishing business.

But do you see the conflict that we have in our own souls? We somehow see the solution: if the whole church of Jesus Christ could get on the move today, then in a few weeks we could reach the entire world with the gospel of Jesus Christ, and the Bible says, "Then the end will come." Most Christians know this as theory, but they don't know what God wants them to do.

What is the type of person that God is going to use? It is the person who asks to hear the truth *whatever the truth may be.* That is the moment when God begins to work in him.

THREE
DON'T MASK
YOUR EMOTIONS

When Nehemiah asked his searching question, he had no idea what information he would get from the men of Jerusalem. But when he heard about the tremendous need of his brethren, he reacted strongly. In chapter 1, verse 4, he recalled, "When I heard these words I sat down and wept, and mourned for days; and I continued fasting and praying before the God of heaven."

How long has it been since you wept? Since you prayed for your Christian brothers who are now being oppressed and persecuted?

In my office I have a small altar where I pray each day when I am in Holland. It has on it a picture of praying hands, and I use the Open Doors prayer reminder which contains pictures of fifty-two believers in prison for their faith. I weep for these brothers as I intercede for them on my knees. I also cry a lot for the countries under the terrible bondage of communism, especially China.

I remember Uncle Hoppy—William Hopkins—my second father, who looked after me when I first arrived in England. Often he used to pray: "Lord, give me the gift of tears." He found it hard to cry; that's why Uncle Hoppy asked so regularly for that gift.

I first learned about weeping when I saw a television film in England with Uncle Hoppy, Corry, and some other friends. It was about the "Great Leap Forward" in China. The BBC program, made entirely on location, was called, "We Must Overtake Britain," and showed people there working like slaves. The slogan on all their lips was, "We must overtake Britain." As I viewed this, the burden of China fell on me, and I began to weep uncontrollably. In fact, it was a long time before I actually got into China. But I think that before anything ever happens, God really has to break the hearts of his children.

I am not saying that we should weep too much in public; and anyway, we can't arrange weeping. But I think that if we really wish to identify with the suffering of our brothers and sisters, even though we may never have seen it, I think the gift of tears will be in operation.

Russian-German pastor Gerhard Hamm, who was imprisoned for many years in the Soviet Union and now works with Open Doors, cries a lot. He weeps from the platform as he tells his story. And when he meets his brothers from concentration camps, they just stand there and hug and weep for ten minutes without saying a word.

Now we come to a problem that is more difficult than weeping for many Christians in the affluent West—fasting. How long has it been since you really fasted? Why do we fast? Is it to support a relief program to starving people? Or do we fast because our spirit is so disturbed about a certain situation that we can't even accept the thought of food?

In Isaiah 58, God lays down his views on real fasting, a deep spiritual involvement that we find in Nehemiah 1. This is the fast that God chooses.

Isaiah 58:3-9 reads: "The people ask, 'Why should we fast if the Lord never notices? Why should we go without food if he pays no attention?' The Lord says to them, 'The truth is that at the same time as you fast, you pursue your own interests and oppress your workers. Your fasting makes you violent, and you quarrel and fight. Do you think this kind of fasting will make me listen to your prayers? When you fast, you make yourselves suffer; you bow your heads low like a blade of grass, and spread out sackcloth and ashes to lie on. Is that what you call fasting? Do you think I will be pleased with that? . . . Remove the chains of oppression and the yoke of

28

injustice, and let the oppressed go free. Share your food with the hungry and open your homes to the homeless poor. Give clothes to those who have nothing to wear, and do not refuse to help your own relatives. Then my favor will shine on you like the morning sun, and your wounds will be quickly healed. I will always be with you to save you; my presence will protect you on every side. When you pray, I will answer you. When you call to me, I will respond'" (TEV).

This is what Nehemiah said: "Here I am." This is also what Jesus said when there was a council in heaven and they were discussing the fate of God's creation. In Hebrews it is recorded: Jesus stepped forth and said, "Here am I, prepare me a body."

Nehemiah's response to the plea for help was in essence to break his fast, share food with the hungry, take the homeless into his house, and clothe the naked when he met them. He would not evade his duty to his kinsfolk.

In fact, Nehemiah was so staggered by the terrible news he heard that he had to grab a chair to sit down. It was too much, and he cried.

To face the revelation of need honestly might be shattering for many. Many would have to sit down and weep. What a wonderful reaction that would be! If our hearts are not sensitive enough to feel pain when we are confronted with need, then I think God can never speak to us.

I ask again; do we ever cry when we hear about a need? "Jesus wept." That's the shortest verse in the Bible, John 11:35. Just two words: "Jesus wept." The apostles wept. And I know cf many great men and women of God who have wept. Have you ever wept over the needs of others? Who is the man that God is going to use? One who can weep for the lost!

Nehemiah mourned and he prayed and he fasted. I once preached at a communion service in a large church in Holland. Having spoken about the suffering Church, I suggested that maybe a time would have to come when the only wine available would be our tears, and the only bread would be our fasting. But what a blessed time that would be! The Bible says that God stores all our tears in his bottle (Psalm 56:8). They are the tears of our prayers. I think God must have many bottles full. One day all that divine power is going to be released and we will see a wonderful work of God's Spirit in the world. And behind it will be the weeping, the praying, and the fasting of all God's people. Make sure that some of your tears reflect the right emotion.

Nehemiah had a very good job and he was happy in his job, but he was a person who would rather know the truth and be unhappy than be happy in ignorance. If we really have spiritually investigative minds, we would want to know the truth, whatever the truth might be, even if knowing that truth would make us unhappy for the rest of our lives. Knowing the truth, however, would make us free to do something about the situation.

So we have to make up our minds that knowing the truth is more important than personal happiness. But then we'll have all of eternity in which to be happy. After all, our main aim for being in the world is not to be happy, but to do the will of God.

The truth about his fellow Jews and about Jerusalem made Nehemiah feel very unhappy. When he wept and fasted and mourned, it was not because he was happy but because he was unhappy. If he had been happy with the news, he would have danced around the place.

I believe that saints are people who can weep before God because something is breaking their hearts. Their ability to weep changes their lives. God then begins to use them.

Nehemiah notes: "Now I was cupbearer to the king" (Nehemiah 1:11). Some people brag about the good jobs they gave up to do the Lord's work, as if the Lord should be very pleased to have them. I think it's mostly exhibitionism, and spiritual pride, because no one has really given up anything.

We don't give up *anything* for God. We misunderstand the cross of Calvary if we even contemplate that Christianity is a sacrifice.

My hero, C.T. Studd, the founder of the Worldwide Evangelization Crusade, once said: "If Jesus Christ be God and died for me, then no sacrifice can be too great for me to make for him."

However, Nehemiah did have a very good position and he knew he would have to give it up; but before he could do this, he would have to speak to the king.

The kings of those days were not the friendly type we have around today. We know from the Book of Esther that even the

queen could not go into the king's room without permission.
And if the queen should go to the king without permission and
it displeased him, she would be killed for doing so.

It was a very risky thing for Nehemiah even to approach the
king about his burden. To be sad in the presence of the monarch
was punishable by death. However, Nehemiah knew that
something had to change in that situation in Jerusalem, just as
you and I know that something has to change in the world
today. No change will come the easy way. You can ask any
revolutionary, any guerrilla fighter, whether in Asia, Africa,
or Latin America. These are people with ideals: they want a
different world, a changed world, and they want it quickly.
But they are all convinced that they will have to pay a price.

Once we begin to understand the blueprint of God for this
world, then immediately we will know that we've got to pay a
price to see that the drastic change he plans becomes a reality.
That's why we speak about "soldiers of Christ." It is a fight; it
is a struggle.

Nehemiah's friends apparently visited him over a weekend,
or while he was on vacation, but now came the day when the
cupbearer had to go back to work. This day, though, something is different. The difference is in the heart of Nehemiah.
He has heard of the need of his people in Jerusalem. In his
heart he can no longer laugh. How I pray that God will make
millions of people different on the inside, through knowing
the truth about the world situation and by getting acquainted
with the plan that God has for this world!

So Nehemiah took the wine and went to the king. It says
that he had never been sad in the presence of the king before. It
was part of his job to cheer him up, so he always had a smile
on his face, whether he meant it or not. Many people are able
to do that. But this time it is different with Nehemiah, because
he knows too much. He cannot put on a smile, even though he
is risking his job, even his life, by coming with a sad face into
the presence of the king.

The king asks, "Why is your face sad, seeing you are not
sick? This is nothing but sadness of the heart."

Nehemiah then admits he is very much afraid. He has come
to an important turning point in his life. He has put his life into
the hands of the king for the sake of God's people. The king

could tell that something sat heavy on Nehemiah's heart. Of course, the thing that was on Nehemiah's heart was what God had put there, and there was no way in which he could disguise it. It was such a strong, divine influence in his life, even the king noticed the difference in Nehemiah.

So often in Christian circles we seem to have a rule: never show your feelings. We don't even show our joy when we know Jesus! I remember when, after a long struggle, I came to know Jesus Christ as my Savior and he lifted the burden of sin. He forgave me all my sin. It was in the dead of winter in 1950 as I lay on my back in bed that I turned my life to God—everything. I just said, "Lord, if you will show me the way, I will follow you. Amen." The implications of the simple prayer hit me the next morning and, as I went out into the cobbled streets of the village where I lived, I couldn't contain my excitement. I spied garbage cans left out for emptying and I jumped over all of those I could find, one by one. It was my expression of joy.

The same week, my neighbor came and asked, "Andrew, what has happened to you?"

"I don't know," I replied, still having the reticence of a good Calvinist not accustomed to speaking of his faith.

"But," he said, "you are different. You look happy."

I later heard about the experience of D.L. Moody, the fiery American evangelist of the last century. One day Moody was doing his topical Bible study on grace and he got so excited about it, that he just ran out into the street, grabbed the first man he came across and said, "Do you know grace?" The bewildered man replied: "Grace who?"

Why do we always try to suppress those feelings of joy? Why do we always try to suppress our feelings of sadness? Why do we never want people to know that we, too, sometimes cry? Are we afraid of looking foolish?

Is every Christian wearing a mask? Can we never show our feelings toward one another? Can we never cry when we hear about a great calamity somewhere?

We profess that we follow Jesus Christ. He was called "the man of sorrows." When Jesus went to the funeral of his friend, Lazarus, he wept. He showed his feelings, his love, his compassion for suffering people. He also showed his anger at unrighteousness.

Why are we so terribly polished? Let's strip away that veneer.

Nehemiah showed his sadness in spite of himself, because of the heavy burden on his heart. His nation was in a state of total collapse; he was living a good life, yet he wanted to be used of God. The remarkable thing is that the king, *because Nehemiah had not masked his emotions*, asked about Nehemiah's burden. And in the end the king gave Nehemiah all his requests for Jerusalem—because he could plainly see the emotional burdens that Nehemiah was carrying.

Let's move ahead a little in the story. Nehemiah has traveled to Jerusalem; he has surveyed the ruined walls of the city at night; but he has never told the people his plans. Finally, he tells them how God's hand had been upon him for good. Immediately the leaders respond to his plans and testimony: "Let us rise up and build," they say (2:18).

There is no greater joy than sharing God's goodness with other people. That is why witnessing Christians are always joyful Christians. There is a proverb I picked up in Russia. It says, "Joy is the same as when you have to sneeze; if you try to suppress your sneeze, then everybody notices it." Don't be ashamed; show your emotions!

Let me tell you something: If you are going to communicate the gospel to people, and you cannot reach their emotions, you cannot lead them to Christ. We say that we follow Jesus. Never was anything great accomplished without great enthusiasm. You ask, "Brother Andrew, is that spiritual?" Yes, it is.

What does the word "enthusiasm" mean? It will surprise you. It means literally, "to be in God."

Now I have a searching question. What about people we meet who are not enthusiastic, yet they say they are in God? I admit I have a problem here. Anyone who is in God should be enthusiastic about that which God has given him to do. In Romans 12:11, there is the injunction, "Be aglow with the Spirit." In the King James Version it says, "Be fervent in Spirit." That is "enthusiasm" in the scriptural sense. If you are always depressed by seeing the world that is broken in pieces, how can you do anything about it? You have to be in God. Then you will have divine enthusiasm working through you, to make you excited about your task.

Let's look at another time when Nehemiah displayed his emotions. After the wall is finished (chapter 13), and the gates are in place, Nehemiah relaxes a bit. But the moment you sit down and relax in your spiritual life, that's the time of danger. In this case, the priest makes a room in the house of the Lord for Tobiah, the enemy of Nehemiah. He takes the enemy from outside right into the camp.

You cannot do that. You cannot fight on two different fronts. That's why the Apostle Paul makes those strong statements in his epistles against sin in the Church. Paul is intolerant toward people who remain living in sin while they profess to be Christians.

You ask how it is possible that the priest could make a room for the enemy of Nehemiah? I know how that can happen! Nehemiah 13:6 says, "While this was taking place I was not in Jerusalem. . . ." While the leader was away, the people did a very foolish thing. What a responsibility we have as followers during times when our leader is away!

When Nehemiah returned to Jerusalem and discovered the evil the priest had done, he said, "I was very angry." Nehemiah saw the big rooms beautifully furnished for his enemy. He opened the windows and threw out all the chairs and all the tables right out onto the street!

My, isn't Nehemiah angry? He sure showed his emotions! Why are we always so nice and kind? We are even nice to the devil! We should not be nice or friendly in the face of satanic opposition. We should be radicals for Jesus and radicals against the devil. Our "No" should be as loud as our "Yes," so that the world knows where we stand. That's the only way to answer satanic opposition, and to continue living effectively for God.

FOUR
"I WANT
THAT
GOLD MEDAL"

In Nehemiah we find an exceptional man who, at the beginning of our story, is doing a secular job. Although he had a good job, as cupbearer to the king, he was still doing something that almost anyone could do. He did not need a special, divine call to be a cupbearer.

But God wanted him to do a special work for his nation, Israel, something that not everybody could do. In other words, God calls people out of the world who are doing something anybody can do, in order to have them do a job that only they can do.

The vast majority of Christians are doing jobs that any person can do. Any person can be a cabdriver, a bookkeeper, or a typist. But only a dedicated follower of Jesus can be a soul winner. Every Christian should ask the Lord, "What do you want me to do?" This attitude is badly lacking in the Christian community worldwide. Christians unfortunately have the same attitude toward life and of getting on in life as non-Christians have. They make exactly the same choices that unbelievers do, and for the same reasons.

Very few Christians ask, "Lord, what do you want me to do?" And yet if we would ask God, he would give us an answer. And we would have a total spiritual revolution in our churches because God has a job for each one of us, a job that no one else can do.

Nehemiah was in exile but doing really well when the brethren came from Judah with bad news. You can almost see the change taking place in Nehemiah; he got the news, then he humbled himself before God and prayed and fasted and wept and mourned. I can see how God then called him, because Nehemiah had brought himself into a place where God could get through to him. But do we understand the elements of his call?

A call is not anything man can give; God has to give it. Yet even God cannot give it if conditions are not right to receive it. But when all these conditions are met, then a marvelous thing happens: a man can do something beyond all human expectations. He can motivate, recruit, and inspire others. The result is that the walls in Jerusalem will be rebuilt.

Why didn't those men who brought in the bad news do anything about it? If you are aware of a certain need, then don't you have to do something about it? Now that may be my activist attitude, which may not be very practical, because I realize there simply are problems that you can do nothing about. There are also separate ministries and diverse responsibilities. It is a corporate, team job to tackle a large task. So you can never say to one, "Why didn't you do something about it?" because that man's sole responsibility may be to tell you about it.

These men were extremely important in fulfilling their communication function; their credibility and their reliability were very important elements used to convince Nehemiah of the need. That was probably their only ministry: to carry the news to a man who at that time still had no call but through the news received a call of God. How important!

Nehemiah was not the only one who had a call. These men had just as much a call, but not to so spectacular a job. Yet if I should have to weigh the importance of the two jobs, I don't know which one was more important. Nehemiah could never have done what he did if these men had not traveled to him and told him. So it is important to be faithful.

The first element of a call from God is the credibility of the information. We, in Open Doors, have a responsibility to make sure that the information we publish on the suffering Church is firsthand. It has to come direct from the believers themselves, whether it be from the Soviet Union, China, or Mozambique. The credibility of the information to Nehemiah was the fact that Hanani accompanied the message direct from Jerusalem. And being a kinsman, Nehemiah knew the information was truly trustworthy.

Nehemiah is an illustration of how the call of God can only reach a man when his heart is open enough to inquire about the needs of others. As long as we are preoccupied with our own problems and ideas and hobbyhorses the Lord will never be able to get through to us with a vision that is bigger than ourselves. An open heart is required before we can ever have a vision to reach someone else, or some other country, or some other continent. We have to be open enough to go looking for the facts.

Nehemiah's heart was also prepared to be sensitive to the need contained in the information.

We need that revelation of need. The first revelation of this kind happened to me when I visited a Bible shop in Warsaw. The director there told me about a professional smuggler who had bought ten Russian Bibles for $50.00 and then smuggled them across the border into Russia. When inside he had made so much money that he bought a brand-new motorbike. He then smuggled it through to Poland, and sold it on the black market for $20,000.

To me the enticing aspect of this piece of free enterprise in Communist territory was not the profit but the revelation of the need—that people would pay that much money for Bibles. I thought, if unbelievers would do that for profit, how much more should we as Christians motivated by need and love for the Lord also do it. But then as a free gift to them.

We have emphasized the negative nature of the need from Jerusalem, but, remember, the people *had* survived! I'm glad that, in Nehemiah's heart, mere survival was not sufficient.

He did not leave it there. He continued to ask searching, honest questions which led, eventually, to a call.

So many people who say they never had a call from God to serve him should really say that they never *heard* the call. When you were a child and you were hungry, you made sure that you were within reach of your mother's voice when she called you for dinner. But if you knew that something unpleasant was waiting for you, you made sure that you were out of reach of her voice. Our attitude, not the strength or fact of the call, makes the difference.

Nehemiah was within reach of the voice that called, so he received the call. Nehemiah was willing to get involved with the things of God. Then God began to call him to do something that no one else could do.

Now every Christian can receive a call like that from God—to do something that no one else can do. Isn't that exciting? Why be a cupbearer for a king when you can have a job with the King of kings!

A willingness to get involved is one of the conditions that we must meet! God cannot and he will not use us if we are not willing to be used.

In addition, God could not get through to Nehemiah until he had confessed his sin. Of course Nehemiah had been speaking to God, but everyone spoke to God. The Pharisees spoke to God, but God never spoke to them. The Jews spoke to God, but God was often unable to respond to them. In many religions, people cry to their gods, but such gods never speak back. But here, Nehemiah speaks to God in confession, and as he confesses his sin he receives cleansing from Almighty God. As he receives divine forgiveness and comes into a right relationship with God, then God begins to speak to him.

Really, isn't that what you want? You want God to speak to you. You want to hear God's voice. Then place yourself in the position where God can speak to you. By making yourself available, by confessing your sins, whatever the consequences will be. Ask him to cleanse your heart and to forgive you. He will do that and prepare you for your call.

Because those messengers from Jerusalem were faithful in reporting to Nehemiah how bad things were there and because Nehemiah humbled himself before the Lord and confessed the sin of his nation and of his father's house and his own sin, at that moment God found a man. Furthermore, Nehemiah immediately related the need in Jerusalem to Almighty God; therefore God gave him faith.

At that time, no one in the entire Middle East had any faith for Jerusalem. As far as the people were concerned, it was written off. The nation of Israel had ceased to exist. The upper classes were all in exile; the poor people had to stay behind and there was no protection for them.

God had let the enemy take over because of the apostasy of his people. But how about the plan of God? How about the place called "Bethlehem"? How about the cross of Calvary? These were still in the plan of God, and for God to see his plan accomplished, something in that situation had to change, even if God could only reach one man.

God did find one man, Nehemiah, who was willing to yield himself to God and to say, "Lord, I don't know what you want of me, but I am available." At that moment God poured faith into Nehemiah. Are you available to do anything God asks you to do?

The Bible says that faith is a gift of God. Never blame God if you have no faith. If faith is a gift of God, you can ask for it. The Bible says, "Ask, and it will be given you" (Matthew 7:7). So if you have no faith, you are the one who needs to take action.

God is looking for a man who will have so much faith that he can impart it to other people. But there will be a price to pay in order to be that person of faith.

Later we see Nehemiah working in Jerusalem. Much has passed in the meantime; much has happened in his own heart. He had done God's will; he did obey God's call, but he is still doing what we could call a secular job. He is building a wall. Why do I point this out? Because there is no such division as secular work and spiritual work. I have warned thousands of young people not to desire to become full-timers in Christian work, because many people think that only then are they something special in the kingdom of God. Actually, there are many unhappy servants of God who would be much happier and more effective if they had stayed in their secular jobs and lived and witnessed for the Lord there.

When I first became a Christian, I was working in a chocolate factory in the Dutch district capital of Alkmaar. I was so enthusiastic, and I won many souls there for Christ. I remember when I first arrived at the factory, which produced high-class bon-bons, many of which were exported to the United States and Germany, I couldn't believe the behavior of the girls there. The dirty jokes and swear words were much worse than I had even heard in the Dutch Army in Indonesia.

"Why do you keep blushing, Andrew? I thought you'd been in the Army," said one girl.

"It was never like this," I replied.

One particularly shy office worker there was Corry, who was later to become my wife. Corry told me that she would watch me witness and live out the Christian life in the boring job that I had been given sorting the chocolates. She said that watching me working hard and enthusiastically at a job that a child aged three could have done encouraged her tremendously and was a witness to the others. Some made inquiries about me and wanted to know what made me different.

In spite of the crude atmosphere in that factory, God did a great work there, and so many eventually came to know Christ that two years later I had to tell some of those same girls not to read their Bibles during working hours. They would even sing hymns as they worked. The transformation on that floor was remarkable. I had never seen anything like it.

I must admit that in those first years of being a full-timer for God I didn't have nearly as much blessing as I used to have in the factory. Many times I prayed to the Lord, "Please send me back to that chocolate factory." I could not understand why I was so unhappy being a full-timer. Now, I am not against young people being full-time in the Lord's work, but I am against the *desire* of young people to be full-timers. You should only go full-time if there is no other way out. It should be as Paul expressed it: "The need is laid upon me, I have no choice" (from 1 Corinthians 9:16, 17.)

When I was working in that chocolate factory back in Holland, I spent every day looking through the factory for people with whom I could talk and witness and pray. Then I thought, "This is not honest; the factory is paying me to work, but I am only working for the Lord." So I left and began living by faith, but that did not make me any happier. And basically it did not make me any more effective, either.

You see, God is preparing our hearts for the highest service. There will never be a time in your spiritual life when God stops preparing you for still higher service. At whatever level you are now, God is still preparing you for higher service. I believe even death is preparation for still higher service, because I don't believe that after you die you stop serving God. For a person with eternal life, service never ends.

There is one specific goal that God has for your life and you must do everything you can to reach it.

In that same chapter in 1 Corinthians, chapter 9, verses 24 through 27, the Apostle Paul compared his life to an athletic race, and he said he did everything he could to train his body and to motivate his spirit because he was determined to win first prize. In other words, if you go to the Olympics, don't tell yourself you will be satisfied with a silver medal; have as your goal only the gold medal. Paul also says that not everybody can win the gold medal. Only one will win that one. But he says you must all have the attitude, "I want that one gold medal!"

When you are gold-conscious, you are not so terribly distracted by the things that you see left and right that have to be corrected. If we are to obey God's call, we must make sure that we are not overly influenced by the statements and criticisms of other people. We must develop a strong character so that, once we've made a decision in the light of the revelation of God, we will not be so easily swayed away from our goal by what people say. We must develop Christian character.

Let me offer you some of my personal thoughts on Christian character. I think that the character of a man is not something that he has when he is born. We speak about the training and development of a Christian worker and we speak about Christian character. We should give God all the glory; it's God's input in man. But God can give us only as much as we allow him to pass on to us. If I yield myself to God, then he can do something with my life; but if I close my heart, and I don't listen to him, I don't read the Scriptures, and I don't fellowship with other spiritual Christians, there is no way in which I can grow into the image of Jesus Christ.

This is a process; it is not something God does in one split second. It will take all the rest of our lives. God constantly works on changing us, and we have to cooperate with God on it. We must, therefore, regularly read the Bible, meditate, pray, and then grow up in him.

Growth is always a process. Let me illustrate this with

three statements that the Apostle Paul made about the state of his own life. There was a time when he said, "For I am the least of the apostles" (1 Corinthians 15:9). Then there comes a time when Paul says, "I am the very least of all the saints" (Ephesians 3:8). Finally, Paul says that he is the greatest of all the sinners (1 Timothy 1:15).

Now these distinct statements trace a progression: the least of all the apostles, the least of all saints, the greatest of all sinners. At what period or sequence of time in his life did Paul make these statements? Now this is most interesting: they come in an exact chronological order! Between the first two statements there are eight years, and then, at the very end of his life, he says that he is the greatest of all sinners. The more he walks with God, the more knowledge he gains about himself, and the more he realizes that he is just nothing; God is everything.

This is what John the Baptist meant when he spoke about Jesus: "He must increase, but I must decrease." Have we already come to that point?

All the good things that are developing in our lives are because of God's input in us, but in some people you simply see more good things than in other people. Is God a respecter of persons? No, he is not, but some people have given God more opportunity to work in their lives. They have enabled God to work more on their character.

What is character? It's the *real* you. It is what you are when you are alone in the dark, not what you are when you stand on the platform or when you sit in a happy group. Everybody can put on a mask, but when you are alone in the dark that's when your real character shows.

Let's again confess: God can do everything. God can change me, and whatever I see God do in other people, he can do in me. Therefore I am going to pray that God will do just that in me.

I go back to the Bible, to Romans 8:32: "He who did not spare his own Son but gave him up for us all, will he not also give us all things with him?"

As we think about the need of the world, as we prepare ourselves for God's service, we have to ask ourselves a few questions: How much has God already done in my life? What are my resources in myself? What can I do in the world? And

one more question: Do I really know what God can do in me?
God can work miracles in my life. God can give or add to my
character so that I can reach my goal.

Sometimes we are so crushed by the burden of the need that
we become ineffective. That is a real possibility. I remember
my first visit to Calcutta, that festering sore that should be on
the conscience of the whole world. There were thousands of
starving people—whole families living out on the sidewalks.
Babies were being conceived, born, and often dying out on the
dirty streets of that terrible Indian city where countless
thousands are homeless. I felt a lump in my throat as scores of
mothers, clutching near-lifeless babies, held out their emaci-
ated hands for money. Their sad, tired eyes made me want to
look away, or even pass by on the other side. But you can't do
that in Calcutta, because there are just as many starving
people across the street.

I remember a similar situation in Indonesia when I was
there with the Dutch Army. As nonbelievers, we soldiers
would step around dying people without real concern because
there was no way we felt we could help them. And even if we
could, we didn't want to. Each morning, big trucks would
come along and pick up the corpses and destroy them.

On my first trip to Calcutta, I could see there was an
obvious solution to the problems there:—communism. The
Christian Church has been in Calcutta for many years, yet the
city is worse than ever. The Communists would be ruthless.
There would be no sacred cows left roaming the streets while
people die of hunger, if they took control.

During that nightmare first visit I realized that already
many of the Indian people had also decided that a Red Revolution was what was needed, and I observed Communist dem-
onstrations in the streets. I hadn't seen so many people carrying Red flags since I had been in places like Red Square,
Moscow, or in Havana, Cuba, after Fidel Castro seized power
there. It scared me because I could see that this could well be
the immediate future of India. I predict that they will have a
Communist revolution and communism will present itself as
the savior because it will solve the social and economic
problems that neither the West, nor the Church, has been
able to do much about. Then they will brag about it and say,

"We saved India." And, in that sense, they will have done that.

When you see tremendous need, and you sense there is nothing you can do about it, there can be real danger that you will just give up, because the need is too great. Even your Christian faith doesn't seem to provide you with an answer for the problems.

The question is, do I relate that need to Calvary, or do I try to find in my own being something to help those people? If I shoulder the responsibility myself, I will be crushed by the burden. I will become ineffective, for I cannot help.

But we have just been confessing that God can do anything! Have I learned to relate the need that I see to Almighty God? Have I so yielded my life to God that he can get through to me with his message? Can he trust me? Can he send me? Can he use me?

I maintain that everything we know about Nehemiah is what God put into him. If God could put all this into Nehemiah, he can put it into you and into me. I refuse any philosophy that says one could do it, but the other could not. God has to do it all. God can use you and he can use me, or Corrie ten Boom, or Billy Graham. It just makes no difference with him. The only difference is that one person says, "Lord, here am I." Then there is no limit with God!

FIVE
"I'M OFF
TO REACH
ANOTHER TRIBE
FOR JESUS"

It is evident that at the time of Nehemiah, God was looking for a man. A few men came from Judah to the place where Nehemiah was living. Nehemiah asked them concerning the Jews that had escaped and concerning Jerusalem. He got a very negative report about his people, so much so that he had to sit down and fast and pray and weep.

God knew the man he wanted. Here was a man with an open heart, a man God needed, one who reacted exactly the way God wanted him to react.

The moment that terrible need came to the mind and heart of Nehemiah, he did the only correct thing—he immediately brought that problem to his God, knowing that only God had the solution. Nehemiah also knew that the way to really get through to God is by prayer and fasting. So he began to pray and fast!

If I have to answer the question, "What kind of person is God using today?" then I would say, "It's the one who humbles himself before God and makes confession of sins."

Then comes the beautiful prayer of Nehemiah in chapter 1, verses 5-11, one of the most moving prayers in the Scriptures. In it he confesses his sin, his father's sin, and his nation's sin. Unless we begin to confess our sin, God will not call us to do anything vital for him.

This is what he prayed: "O Lord God of heaven, the great

and terrible God who keeps covenant and steadfast love with those who love him and keep his commandments; let thy ear be attentive, and thy eyes open, to hear the prayer of thy servant which I now pray before thee day and night for the people of Israel thy servants. . . ."

He first acknowledges that God's ears and eyes are open. God knows what's happening in the world today. If anybody's heart in this universe is broken about the need in the world, it is his heart, because he sees all the needs in the world. And I am convinced that God has an answer to every question and a solution to every need for every person in the world. Oh, what a big heart God must have!

Nehemiah then describes himself as God's servant. Now that is the right attitude, because when a man comes as a servant, it means that he is willing to accept orders. So many people come to Christian leaders and say they want to do something, but in their own minds they have a whole list of things they are not willing to do. For our own work, we always have difficulty finding people who are willing to do all the dirty jobs that have to be done.

Are we really willing to take orders, to do anything? Have you ever heard of that great missionary, C.T. Studd? A former English international cricketer, Studd was the founder of the Worldwide Evangelization Crusade. He had been a member of the "Cambridge Seven" who went out from England to form a strong evangelistic team to work with Hudson Taylor in China. Studd had been a very wealthy man, but he gave up everything for Jesus. He literally got rid of all he owned, and the Lord used him greatly in China. Because of his relentless labors and sacrificial living there, he became seriously ill. He was so sick that the doctors called him "a museum of tropical diseases."

Actually, C.T. Studd came back to England a broken man.

One day he was walking in town and saw an announcement for a missionary rally. The notice said, "Cannibals Need Missionaries." He laughed at the implications of that wording, but still he went to the rally. There God called him to be a missionary to Africa.

He was already a grandfather, and still a desperately sick man, but he went to the heart of Africa, where no missionary had ever been. He worked day and night to give the native people the gospel. During the seventeen pain-racked years he worked in Africa, he did not go home on furlough once. In those years he saw his wife Priscilla only one time. He loved her, his children, and his grandchildren, but he wanted them to be in Britain to organize the home front—the prayer force.

I have talked to a number of people who worked with Studd in Africa and I have heard some amazing stories about that man. Such an inspiring life! He was always looking for people who could take over for him, but he was a very hard master. He had forsaken everything for the Lord, and he demanded the same of his followers. He had a right to do that. You cannot ask anyone to do that which you have not done yourself, but he had done it all.

Because of the pain he was experiencing near the end, C.T. Studd was often given pain-killing drugs to help him continue. His personal attendant, Jimmy Taylor, a Baptist, was there with him. One night he thought that Studd was definitely dying, so he went over at eleven o'clock to give him a couple of shots to kill the pain and knock him out, so the great missionary could sleep.

At about 3:00 A.M., Taylor became concerned and thought he had better go and check to see if Studd was still alive. When he arrived at the hut where Studd lived, he was shocked to find it empty. On the table were pages with writing and a little note. It read: "Dear Jim, I have translated a couple more chapters of Acts and I am off now on my bicycle to reach another tribe for Jesus. They have never heard of him."

This was just four hours after he had been given his "last" shots. Nobody could follow C.T. Studd. His steps were far too big. He really had no followers. Almost all of his co-workers left him in despair because they couldn't keep up with him.

Shortly before his death he called in his daughter, who had come to visit him in Africa, and said he would like to give her something in memory of her father. He looked around his hut and then said, "I have nothing left. I have given everything to Jesus." Can we say that?

One man by the name of Harrison wanted to help C.T. Studd in the missionary work in Africa, but Studd had him work all day on carpentry and repairing shoes. For two full years he worked only with his hands. Now, Harrison could have done that back in England and made good money doing it, but he did the same simple jobs in Africa because in his heart he was doing it for Jesus. When C.T. Studd died, Harrison did become his successor—because he was willing to be a servant.

Most people are willing only to be preachers. We want to stand in front of people and preach. If you ask us to dig in the garden, we say, "The Lord did not call me to do that." That may be true, but God *did* call you to be a servant, and the servant always obeys. God may let you dig in the garden for ten years, but he will use that time to prepare you for that one moment of supreme service.

There may come a moment in your life when you will be able to reach a whole city or nation in one day. Only on that day will you understand why you had to occupy the servant's role through all the years of your life.

This was the attitude of Nehemiah. He knew that a servant is one who is willing to obey the master. There is no sense in your praying for the world if you are not willing to be a servant, because basically you have to be willing to be the servant of the person to whom you are going to present Christ.

As a messenger of Jesus, you come in the role and attitude of a servant. That's why Jesus said, "Don't let yourself be called 'Rabbi.'" Don't be a master, don't be a lord; be a servant, for as you are a servant of all, then you can minister to all.

Remember that Nehemiah had a high position in the palace of the king, yet he knew that in relation to God and man he was a servant. That is one of the things that is required before God can use you.

Nehemiah goes on in his prayer with a confession of sin. He continues (in verse 6), ". . . confessing the sins of the people of Israel, which we have sinned against thee. Yea, I and my father's house have sinned." Unless there is a confession of sin, there is no forgiveness of sin. If there is no forgiveness of sin there is no liberty to witness about Jesus Christ. If there is anything that silences the believer, it is unconfessed sin in his life.

Nehemiah also confessed the sin of his nation. Now I think that's quite easy to do. It's always so easy to say, "We have sinned." But we have to go a step further and say, "I am a sinner, because I have sinned." And if I have sinned it means I am a sinner, even when the Word of God says I am a saint. If you have let sin come back into your life and you have not confessed it, then today you are a sinner and God cannot use you to the fullest possible extent.

I am not going to say that God does not use you at all. God will use everyone. When Jonah ran away from the call of God instead of going to Nineveh to preach the gospel there, he ran away on a ship going to Tarsus. Even though he was disobedient and was living in sin, God used him on that ship. The crew were heathen people, but it says that after they heard what Jonah's business was and what his sin was, then they began to pray to the only true God. So even through his disobedience, Jonah was a blessing to perhaps twenty people on that ship.

God can always use you. But think of what God could really do if you were not living with your sin! So if there is any sin unconfessed in your life, even though you realize that God is still using you, do not let that small blessing be an excuse for not putting things right with God. If you would get right with God and with man, God might use you ten or a hundred times more than he is now. Do you want that? Your main concern should always be that there be nothing between God and you. Then whatever God has for you he can give you in his good time.

I remember back in July, 1953, the Lord convicted me of boyhood sins that I had actually forgotten about. I realized how they were coming between me and his blessing. I was in Glasgow, with my English friend Uncle Hoppy, at a Wesleyan Holiness convention. I earnestly sought the power of the Holy Spirit in my life. I knew that I needed it to progress as a Christian.

As I was asking the Lord to fill me with the Holy Spirit, he brought to my memory unconfessed sins that, as a boy, I had committed. The first "crime" took place against my older brother Ben, of whom I was then very jealous. I had always thought he was given special treatment by my parents because he was the eldest. Ben had the nicest cupboard and clothes; he also had much more money than I, and I knew he kept it all in a piggy bank in his bedroom. One day, while he was out, I got hold of his bank and began to shake out the coins. Then I reported to the local police that I had found some money on the street. There was a law then that the finder could keep what was found, and if it was not claimed within a year, it would become his or her property. I did this regularly and soon amassed a small fortune.

I had completely forgotten my "crime," but as I was seeking the Holy Spirit there in that Scottish city, it came flooding back. It was as if God told me, "Andrew, you cannot get more from me unless you first confess your sin." So I wrote a long letter to my brother admitting my thieving and asking him for forgiveness. I also told him I was going to repay him. I received a beautiful letter back from Ben.

"Andrew," he wrote, "there is nothing to forgive or pay back; the only debt we have to each other is to love each other."

At the same time, the Lord reminded me of an occasion during the war when I had stolen apples. There was a big farm near my home that had thousands of crates of this succulent fruit. I couldn't get the complete apples out, so I would cut slices through the opening in the crates and then eat them. I determined that I would go back to the firm on my next furlough and make reparation. The boss of the company was surprised when I confessed to my wartime exploits, especially when I offered to pay ten times the amount that I thought I had stolen.

I told the owner that I was now a Christian and that was the reason for my action.

The owner turned to me and said, "Oh my! I have never heard this. I wish we had time to talk about God." He let me off.

I then went back to a shop where I had stolen cigarette lighters and pocket knives when I was about twelve years old. I confessed to the proprietor, who gratefully received my compensation.

"If everybody would do that for what has been stolen from here over the years, I could close the shop and become a millionaire," he said.

I had committed those boyhood wrongs and then put them

right and confessed and repaid. It was quite an experience. And it certainly brought me closer to the Lord.

Nehemiah saw how sin in his nation, in his church, in his family, and in his life had made him inactive for the Lord. The hardest confession of all is to say, "I have sinned," for then you have to tell God what you did. Nehemiah said (in verse 7), "We have acted very corruptly against thee, and have not kept the commandments, the statutes and the ordinances which thou didst command thy servant Moses." In other words, he is confessing the sin of omission.

It is much easier, in my opinion, to confess sins which you commit, because you become the first victim of the sin. You lose your peace with God because of the sins you commit. It is harder to confess sins of omission—the things you should have done but did not do. These sins cause problems for other people, but you don't feel their pain. Perhaps that's why we lack courage to ask about others' problems. Basically, all the problems of the world are a result of our not keeping his commandments.

As long as I live, I will continue to preach the Great Commission. In that, Jesus gave the solution to all the problems of the world. But we have not kept his commandments; we have not gone into all the world; we have not made the gospel available to all nations. There are still 3,000 tribal groups that do not have one verse of Scripture in their languages. Do you know that there are more illiterate people in the world today than ever before in history? There are also, in sheer numbers, more people unreached with the gospel than ever before in these 2,000 years of Christianity. More nations today than ever before will not allow missionary work. A number of countries do not have a national church within their borders. Places like Afghanistan, Saudi Arabia, Mongolia, North Korea, Libya, Yemen, Tibet, and Albania. Mongolia had fellowships before World War II, and Albania had a small group of American missions working on the Greek border, but they pulled out in 1938 with the only known Albanian Christians. We in Open Doors have not been able to find one believer in Albania, despite several visits by our staff. Afghanistan has never had a national church, nor has Saudi Arabia or Yemen.

Why? Because God's people had not kept his commandments. This is exactly what Nehemiah is confessing.

I think the sins of omission are probably far, far bigger than the sins we commit, but there is a very subtle difference. You may be guilty of the grossest sins of omission and remain a very respectable person. I think that's exactly our problem. We can appear to be the most moral, spiritual people, but in the sight of God we are the worst sinners because we have not done what Jesus told us to do.

You may have read the book, *God's Smuggler*. I feel very sad that it ever had to be written. More than twenty-five years ago, when the events in the book took place, not one mission was working in Communist countries. Why did that book have to be written? Because the work that I was doing was then exceptional, and people wanted to read about it. If 5,000 people had been doing the same ministry, then nobody would think about writing such a book.

Do you see my point? If we had obeyed the commandments of Jesus Christ, then we would never have neglected all those so-called "closed" countries. Then many churches and missionaries would have been going there *all the time*.

Nehemiah continues his prayer (verses 8 and 9), "Remember the word which thou didst command thy servant Moses, saying, 'If you are unfaithful, I will scatter you among the peoples; but if you return to me and keep my commandments and do them, though your dispersed be under the farthest skies, I will gather them thence and bring them to the place which I have chosen, to make my name dwell there.'"

Note that God's promises are always conditional. Nothing that is recorded in the Bible will happen just because it is written in the Bible. God always cooperates with his people, if his people are faithful.

Nehemiah prays, "They are thy servants and thy people, whom thou has redeemed by thy great power and by thy strong hand" (v. 10). He is simply pleading on the basis of the Word of God. Nehemiah didn't even know where all those people lived! He hadn't even known what was happening in Jerusalem, and that was the Holy City with the remains of the temple! But in faith he claims all of the nation for God.

Faith is now pouring into the heart of Nehemiah. As he

prays to his God, he can already see his people redeemed, even though he knows the walls of Jerusalem are broken down, the gates burned, the people in great trouble and shame. That is what his physical eye sees, but his spiritual eye sees the people redeemed. Are the physical and spiritual realities too contrasting? Not necessarily. All that God needs is to put man in between—a man or a woman of God—to bring the two together.

Let us read again in that prayer (verse 11): "O Lord, let thy ear be attentive to the prayer of thy servant, and to the prayer of thy servants who delight to fear thy name; and give success to thy servant today, and grant him mercy in the sight of this man." He has now brought the need to his God. He has made himself available to bridge the gap between what he sees by faith and what his physical senses tell him. He is openly praying for success!

Do we ever literally pray for success? We ask for blessings, and very often I fear people take success to be a blessing. But success is not always blessings, and blessings are not always success.

Success is usually what you can measure with your eyes and with your mind; blessing is that which happens in the kingdom of God. When Jesus Christ died on the cross, it didn't look like success, yet in God's sight it was. When we lay down our lives for the world, that may not look like success either, but it's the only way we can be a blessing to the world. That is the type of blessing which, in the kingdom of God, means success. Do you want that? Nehemiah was offering himself to be a blessing. Now he is a man God can use.

SIX
THE LIFE
OF PRAYER

Nehemiah was, above all, a man of prayer. Whenever he was confronted with a problem, his immediate reaction was to take it to the Lord in prayer. Isn't that very much like the character of Jesus? Wasn't the Lord often found in prayer? Even late in the evening, after he had sent his disciples home, Jesus went up into the mountain to pray. While the disciples were enjoying a good night's sleep, Jesus was out there on the mountain, alone, praying.

Now let us look more closely at Nehemiah's prayer reaction. In the very first chapter of his book, when he heard the bad news from Jerusalem, it says that he sat down, wept, mourned, and then continued fasting and praying before the God of heaven. We have already examined his beautiful prayer of confession.

Is our first reaction, when we hear about a need, to relate it in prayer to God? If we do not do that, I doubt that God will then tell us to do anything about that particular need.

Recently, I became acutely aware that I needed more time alone with the Lord. I had to ask my secretary and other personnel to move from my back-garden office. The decision wasn't popular with my staff, who now have moved to our headquarters in Ermelo. But it had to be done.

Often at night I would return to the office to pray and be alone with the Lord and would find people still there. I need to pray aloud or cry or read, and so absolute privacy is vital. So now, sadly, they've all gone.

I think, for every man of God, it is absolutely essential that he has a place where he can be alone. That's why Abraham went into the field and God said, "Your offspring will be like the stars that you have been gazing at."

Jacob had to go out alone at night to the brook where the angel of God wrestled with him. That's where his name Jacob was changed to Israel.

Moses went alone to the Tent of the Lord's Presence. God would never have met him in the camp.

Beware of the barrenness of a busy life. One of the tricks of the devil for any man of God is to make him busy. That way you miss the point, or as I said earlier, you will never be able to reach a nation in one day. God may take a lifetime of preparation to use a man for one supreme moment of service. John the Baptist had that moment of glory, and became the greatest of all the prophets that one day when he introduced Jesus to the people. He told the crowds, "Behold the Lamb of God, who takes away the sin of the world" (John 1:29).

In Luke 7:24, Jesus said that John the Baptist was the greatest of all the prophets. This only came about because of the time and preparation and loneliness John went through. He paid the price.

Being alone with the Lord is a constant problem for me when I am traveling. I will arrive in a hotel after a long flight and will be tempted to turn on the television and unwind there in front of the box before my next meeting. The temptation is worst in the United States because there are so many Christian programs on the air. Once I have turned that knob, I am hooked, so my only salvation is not to switch it on at all.

I pray, "Lord, give me an open heaven in this place." Then I can have a good time with him, but I have to fight for it.

In chapter 2, Nehemiah faced the king, and the king asked why he was so sad. Nehemiah began to explain about the problems of Jerusalem, and immediately the king asked, in effect, "What do you want of me? What is your request?" As Nehemiah recounts that incident, he says, "So I prayed to the God of heaven. And I said to the king. . . ."

Can you imagine Nehemiah and the king carrying on this

conversation? The king, that all-powerful potentate, has asked Nehemiah what he wants him to do. What do you think Nehemiah will do? Is he going to look in his notebook to see what it is he should ask of the king? Is he going to go into a corner, drop on his knees, and pray to God?

This is a heathen king who has asked a very straightforward question. He expected an immediate answer and he got one. Note what Nehemiah did. "So I prayed to the God of heaven. And I said to the king. . . ." That's what I call a telegram prayer. It was so short the king never noticed it.

Do you believe in telegram prayers? I do. I have used them on all my border crossings. Obviously there is no way I could get on my knees and have a session of prayer while a guard is checking my luggagge and car. So this is my way of making instant contact with the Lord.

One day when I really needed a telegram prayer was when I was in the center of Moscow with Rolph, a colleague. We were in a big delivery van in which I had made panels in the rear and all along the sides to cover our cargo of 800 Bibles. The only way I could get those Bibles out in Moscow was to drill out hundreds of pop rivets and then slip out the whole panels.

I told Rolph to keep driving around the Russian capital as I worked feverishly at my task. We had Dutch plates on the car and could have been stopped at any moment by the police, especially because of the way that Rolph was careening through red lights.

"Not so fast," I told him, perspiration pouring from all over me. He just kept going, his foot down on the gas pedal, lurching from Red Square to the suburbs and back again. All the time I kept drilling out those pop rivets.

Suddenly Rolph screeched to a halt and from my vantage point behind the wafer-thin curtain, I heard a voice bark in Russian, probably saying something like, "You have just committed a traffic violation."

I realized immediately that it was a policeman. In an instant I shot up a telegram prayer. "Lord," I whispered, "please blind his eyes."

I knew that humanly speaking we were well and truly caught. I had already taken some of the panels off and was filling up my old rubber canoe with our contraband Scriptures.

Rolph kept chattering away to the officer in Dutch, which obviously confused the man, while I sat in the back hardly daring to breathe.

After a little lecture—of which of course we didn't understand very much at all—he hissed, "Get going. . . ." Rolph smiled at the man, started up the engine and soon we were off again on our lurching journey around Moscow, this time at a slightly slower pace. Soon I had all the Bibles out, and then began popping the new rivets back in and painting over them. It wasn't long before our hair-raising journey was over and the Bibles were in the hands of grateful believers of Moscow's underground church.

As we handed over the Bibles at a prearranged spot, I said, "Thank you, Lord. You answered our telegram prayer."

I believe, however, that God answers them only on one condition. That is that you take time for prayer *when you have the time.* Don't forget that for several days before Nehemiah met the king, he had spent his time in prayer and fasting, in weeping and confession.

This gives us again a marvelous insight into the character of Nehemiah. He brings his need to the heart of God. This is the only way in which we can effectively carry the burden. If we try to carry the burden alone, it will kill us. If we do not bring the burden to God, we are ineffective. Nehemiah is our beautiful example here.

Nehemiah was simply a man of prayer. That was the divine character that God had put in his life and that's the reason that God could use him so greatly. God knew how he would react as he faced the king. And so much depended on the right response. If Nehemiah had not been a man of prayer, and had given a wrong answer, then the future of Jerusalem would have been affected by it.

One quick answer or one quick action of ours could well have a tremendous impact on the world situation. Do we know how to be "instant in prayer" as Nehemiah was?

That, again, is why we need to study the Bible constantly. There are so many prayers recorded there, and the stories of so many people of prayer from whom we need to learn.

We can learn so much from Nehemiah. In chapter 4, he prays, "Hear, O our God, for we are despised; turn back their taunt upon their own heads, and give them up to be plundered in a land where they are captives. Do not cover their guilt, and let not their sin be blotted out from thy sight; for they have provoked thee to anger before the builders" (vv. 4,5).

This is one of those very practical prayers. Enemies have threatened to stop the work. One prayer to God does not always solve the problem or take away satanical opposition. So, too, here in Jerusalem the opposition continues, and in the same chapter, verse 9, it says, "And we prayed to our God, and set a guard as a protection against them day and night." They prayed and they worked. But first they prayed, and God must have given them an answer. It would appear that God himself had issued the order: put guards around for protection!

In chapter 6, verse 9, there is a different kind of prayer. Nehemiah is speaking to his enemies, and all of a sudden he prays, "But now, O God, strengthen thou my hands." In other words, he is suddenly aware of his own inadequacy to handle the situation. He is just too weak to solve the particular problems of that moment so he turns to God. He immediately relates that need to God in an ejaculatory prayer!

In the same chapter, verse 14, there is one more prayer. Nehemiah is talking again about the attempts of his enemies to stop the work. Suddenly he prays, "Remember Tobiah and Sanballat, O my God, according to these things that they did, and also the prophetess Noadiah and the rest of the prophets who wanted to make me afraid." Nehemiah's instant response to the threat of these people was to pray about it.

We must realize the import of Nehemiah's struggle. A lot was at stake! If he had not been able to build the wall to protect the Temple and the houses, then Christmas would not have taken place. That may seem a strange thing for me to say, but it's true. The Temple had to continue functioning for the religious aspect of Judaism to keep on producing priests and prophets, so that one day Zechariah could hear from the angel concerning John the Baptist and the birth of Jesus. Jerusalem, as a city, had to continue in order that the national identity, with this great city at its center, could eventually spread out over the whole country. That then meant that the Emperor Augustus could issue his decree that everyone had to go to his own birthplace to be registered. It was only through this unspoken chain of events that Joseph and Mary could have traveled to Bethlehem for the birth of their son.

All this was at stake with the rebuilding of Jerusalem. So the attacks on Nehemiah were definitely a satanic attempt to prevent the rebirth of a Jewish nation so that Jesus Christ could not then be born in Bethlehem, the event about which all the prophets had spoken.

We read in chapter 2, verse 10: "When Sanballat the Horonite and Tobiah the servant, the Ammonite, heard this, it displeased them greatly that someone had come to seek the welfare of the children of Israel." The Ammonite was, of course, one of the relatives of Abraham, as was Sanballat and the Arabs mentioned in the book. In fact, Arabs are just as much sons of Abraham as the Jews. It is a sad but true fact that the counterfeit religionists are nearly always the severest enemy of the true servants of God. It's not the atheists, as we usually think. I believe communism is not the biggest enemy we face but rather apathy and false teaching inside the Church.

These people also opposed Nehemiah because they were not of the same spirit. Nominally religious people will always persecute the saints. Now, as always, the fiercest attacks come from the counterfeit church.

It is interesting to see that in the Communist countries, they purposely employ ceremonies which they have copied from the Christian Church. Instead of confirmation, they have the Jugend-Weihe. And they have a substitute in communism for all the Christian emblems and ceremonies, because they know that is the way to kill the real thing.

The crazy thing is that the devil is not very original. He always has the same dirty tricks. If you know one, you know them all. That's why it is important that we should know more about the "roaring lion."

Then in chapter 9 we read about another prayer. In this chapter, Nehemiah has gathered a group of co-workers around himself, and he commissions them to do certain tasks. In effect, he is delegating some of his responsibilities, and asks them to "stand up and bless the Lord." In this case it is not just the problem that he brings to God, but now that God has answered earlier prayers and has given him co-workers, he brings these co-workers to God.

The prayer in chapter 9 is a beautiful prayer spoken by the Levites, probably under the direction of the prophet Ezra. This very long prayer stretches from verse 5 through verse 37. There are three unusual prayers in the Old Testament that seem particularly helpful if you are spiritually dried up and need revival in your life. They are easy to remember, because each occurs in a chapter 9. They are found in Ezra 9, Nehemiah 9, and Daniel 9. There is so much spiritual insight in these prayers that it will bring revival to your own heart, if you will read them on your knees and say, "Lord, make these three prayers true in my own life."

Since the prayer in chapter 9 is by the Levites, I will not comment further on it. We find Nehemiah praying again in chapter 13, verses 14, 22, 29, and 31. These are simply prayers that come in the midst of his busy program. He speaks about problems and plans, and suddenly he prays a short exclamatory prayer. It is evident that his was a life characterized by communion with God in prayer.

When I look at Nehemiah, I see a great man of prayer. A common theme in his prayer life is that need drove him to God. In almost every instance, Nehemiah prayed because of the tremendous crushing burden of the need. If a need would crush a person, that person would become useless; so the moment a need comes to you, you must relate it to God in prayer. Then I think God will show you what you can do about the situation.

Prayer brought Nehemiah to a place where he could hear the voice of God. As he prayed, God said, "Do something about it." Had he never prayed, had he simply bemoaned his state and his terrible enemies, God would never have used him. But he found the right place in prayer, humbling himself, so that God could use him.

Nehemiah was a man of prayer, but he was also a man of courage, and I think the two go together, because if you are a man of prayer it means that you know God, and if you know God there is nothing you have to be afraid of. There is a very beautiful verse in Nehemiah chapter 6, verse 11. A message has come to Nehemiah that his enemies are going to kill him, and his friends say, "Please, Nehemiah, run for your life!" Nehemiah replies, "Should such a man as I flee?"

Really, in our own hearts, we would all like to run away from big problems. You see that happening all through the Bible. When Israel was facing the Philistine army and their big champion, Goliath, everyone in Israel had the tendency to run. There was only one young boy who knew his God. He had often spoken to his God; he had done great things for his God, but nobody had seen him, because he had been alone with the flock. He had fought with a bear and a lion because of the personal responsibility he felt for his father's sheep. And because he had been faithful in the little things that were entrusted to him, he was going to be faithful when he saw the biggest threat to the life of his nation that day. Somewhere in the heart of David was the same reaction as we see here with Nehemiah. "Should such a man as I flee?"

He said to King Saul, "Let me have a go at that giant." And to Goliath he said, "The battle is the Lord's and he will give you into our hand" (1 Samuel 17:47).

That courage comes only from an intimate knowledge of our God.

An exact present-day analogy we can draw from this story is that we, in the West, are as petrified of the Russians as the Israelites were afraid of Goliath. We see communism as our number one enemy—as they saw the giant as their's. In 1 Samuel chapter 17, verse 25, we read, "The men of Israel said (to David), 'Have you seen this man . . .?'" They were pointing out how big and strong he looked. He was a menacing threat to them.

But David looked at him and said, "Who is this uncircumcised Philistine, that he should defy the armies of the living God?" David didn't see the problem but rather the greatness of God.

What makes me and my teams go into the Communist countries? It is the same conviction that David had: the greatness of God has preserved the suffering Church. They are like the remnant left in Jerusalem, whom Nehemiah went to help. Our ministry in a nutshell is to strengthen what remains and is ready to die.

As we look at the Church of Jesus Christ in the Communist countries, we then have to put the problem into the right theological context. That is what David did. Then our eyes are no longer on the big enemy, as is the case especially in America. I think of the plethora of anti-Communist preachers in the United States who spend all their time and energy fighting communism. Their crusade, they believe, is to save America from this threat. But I say they are wrong. As long as you fight communism, you are paralyzed with fear. And you can't win. All the people today who fight against the devil are losers, because he has more experience then we have.

All we have to do is hide behind the Cross, let Jesus do the fighting, and rest in what he has done on Calvary. That is the basic Christian message. But, still, people don't understand, and they struggle and lose.

David puts the situation into the right theological context when he says that this uncircumcised Philistine has no place or right in the kingdom of God. This is what enables us to get into Communist countries or any of the so-called "closed" countries: we seek the Church, and in seeking it, we look for the Body of Christ which no one can destroy. We don't look at the problem, but we get our eyes fixed on the greatness of God and that enables us to get in.

David had no fear when he took on Goliath. Similarly, we do not turn into Jell-O when we pass through hostile borders. That is not because we are so courageous, because we are not. My definition of courage, by the way, is not the absence of fear, but the pressing on in spite of it.

Later, in verse 45, David said to Goliath, "You come to me with a sword and with a spear and with a javelin; but I come to you in the name of the Lord of hosts. . . ." He announced himself far superior because of the One behind him. That's what makes me feel so good when I go into the restricted countries.

There's no self-elevation here because this is a confession of faith. The real reason behind it all is that I have come in the name of the Lord of hosts.

As David says in verse 46, "That all the earth may know that there is a God in Israel." This is the purpose for which we do it: to expose the weakness of the powers of evil, and to proclaim the infallible Word of God and the ultimate victory of Jesus Christ. He shall reign from sea to sea and pole to pole. There shall be no end to his kingdom. All the earth will know there is a God, and that is what makes the work so exciting.

When I have traveled in Communist countries, I have often met young people who wanted to leave their countries. They wanted to go to the "free" West, preferably to America. I always said, "Don't do it. If you know God, you should not flee. You must stay here and serve God, because you can only fight for God where there are enemies of God. If you flee from the battlefield, if you shun the conflict, then you come into an area where you may not have the divine protection on your life any more."

Fortunately, many people have listened to me; they stayed in their countries and today are effective witnesses for Jesus. But many of those who left their countries and went to America are backsliders today. If God gives us his courage, then we will be able to stand any amount of opposition. We will never be afraid of the enemy.

Some years ago, I spoke at a conference in Havana on the subject outlined in John chapter 10: that a shepherd is not to leave his sheep or he becomes a hireling. At the end of the sermon, a well-groomed man, who turned out to be a pastor, stood up. "Brother Andrew," he told me in front of the hushed congregation, "I have been planning to leave Cuba for America. I already have my application papers being processed at the moment, but after what I have heard you say about a shepherd staying with the flock, I have decided before God tonight to stay."

The people rose as one and clapped their hands. They said, "Gracias, Padre; O gracias, Padre." They were so happy. This man stayed and was greatly used of the Lord there in Cuba, in that difficult situation.

I have been urged by many, including people from the Pentagon in Washington, to get out of Holland and retreat to somewhere less accessible. They have told me I am in danger from the Russians because of my work.

"Brother Andrew, you must be at the top of their hit list," said one military man from the United States. I told him, "If I run for my life, then the devil would catch up with me. I can only have God's full protection if I stay in the center of his will. And after all, it would be a terrible example to those who risk their lives by staying and working in those 'closed' countries if I ran for safety."

I *will not move*, because I believe we should all stay in the place where God places us and also in the place of responsibility.

I repeat with Nehemiah, "Should such a man as I flee?"

Think again about the story of Nehemiah. There were thousands of people in need in Israel. They were all aware of their need. Most of them were probably praying every day to God about the need . . . yet nothing happened. They may even have begun to think that God does not answer prayer.

When does the change come? When one man gives up his rights and privileges and brings his need to God! In other words, when that man becomes a mediator. God has called every believer to be a prophet and a priest. What is a priest? A priest is one who stands between God and man. The moment you make intercession for another person, at that moment you are a priest. A priest is one who lays one hand on the shoulder of man and the other hand on the throne of God. He brings the two into contact with each other and he does not let go of either one of them until he has seen the results.

That is what Nehemiah did. He stood between the need of Israel and the Almighty God; he had a genuine concern for the welfare of his people.

Prayer should be the believer's most expected spiritual reaction. Through it, God calls people into involvement. We should never feel bad about people promising only to pray, because we know prayer is the first step toward fuller involvement. By prayer, God opens up the whole picture, so that we see what the enemy is doing, and we see the importance of our contribution.

SEVEN
ARE YOU
SHOCKPROOF?

Nehemiah was a man of great foresight. He obviously knew something about strategy, and he planned well. Just when he realized that he was the one who should rebuild the walls of Jerusalem is difficult to say. We know he did not tell any of his Jewish friends until after he had been in Jerusalem several days. But that goal had been very clearly in his view for some time.

During his interview with the king, in chapter 2, verse 8, he makes sure that he gets a letter addressed to Asaph, "the keeper of the king's forest, that he may give me timber to make beams for the gates of the fortress of the temple, and for the wall of the city, and for the house which I shall occupy." Nehemiah knew what he needed to ask for, and why he needed to ask for it.

God wants to use us in his work, there is just no doubt about that. Every Christian individual is called to work for God. But before you can work for God you have to know what you are going to work on.

Let me give a very plain illustration. If you're going to work at a construction site where they're going to build a house, and you tell the foreman you are a bricklayer or a carpenter, and he hires you, then what do you do? You don't just begin to work anywhere. If you're a bricklayer, you don't just begin to put bricks on a pile; or if you're a carpenter, you don't just take hammer and nails and fasten some wood together. That would never make a house.

You first have to see the blueprint. You must have a plan; you must know what you're going to do and why you're going to do it. You must know your place in the team of people who together are going to build that particular house.

Now this is a very important principle in Christian work, perhaps one of the most overlooked principles. Workers never seem to know their role in God's strategy. They think that the highest job in the world is to win a few souls for Christ, but that may mean they haven't looked into God's plan, that they have not studied the strategy of the kingdom of God.

There is one theme that runs through the whole Bible. Beginning in the first two chapters of Genesis, we know that God has a plan by which he wants to defeat the enemy and that the means by which God is going to do it is through his people. God is going to use people to defeat the devil and his whole demon host, and somewhere in the process he is going to send his Son from heaven to enable the church that will be formed at that time to utterly crush the devil. Now that is the shortest synopsis I can give of the whole Bible.

All through the entire Old Testament, God is leading his people up to that one moment when, in Bethlehem in a stable, his Son will be born. All the attacks of the devil in the Old Testament are intended to prevent the plan of God by which Jesus is to be born in Bethlehem.

So many Old Testament events relate in a negative way to that night when Jesus had to be born in Bethlehem. For instance, the fact that the brothers of Joseph sold him into slavery was not just a means of getting rid of Joseph; it was the devil's attack to make impossible the birth of Jesus Christ. All the attacks of enemies upon the nation of Israel relate to the birth of Jesus in Bethlehem. The devil tried every possibility to prevent that from happening.

God has always had a blueprint. That's why the Bible says, in Ezekiel, chapter 22, verse 30, "And I sought for a man among them who should build up the wall and stand in the breach before me for the land, that I should not destroy it; but I found none." God looked for a man, but there were times in Israel when the light had almost gone out. In 1 Samuel we read there was a time when God was not speaking anymore in Israel. The light had almost gone out in Israel, but there was still one little boy named Samuel who could hear the voice of God. He led his nation back to God.

To think that one person can be so important in the plan of God! That's why we must think big, we must see God's plan in global, historic terms. God used individuals all through history to make it possible one day for his Son to be born in Bethlehem. Until the very last minute, the devil tried to prevent the birth of Jesus. That's why Jesus was born in the night, surrounded by a host of angels who were there not just to sing to the shepherds in Bethlehem but also to preserve the life of Jesus Christ, who that night descended from heaven into this world.

When Jesus was born, the devil made one more attack to kill that baby. The devil used three astrologers from the Far East to go to King Herod to betray the baby. I personally think that these three so-called "wise men" were very occult men. They got their guidance from the stars, as millions of people do today. That's why they went to the wrong place. Their confidence in astrology did not lead them to the stable; it led them to the palace of King Herod. It gave Herod the opportunity to kill all the babies in Bethlehem. You see how all of hell combined with mankind in an attempt to kill the life of Jesus Christ.

The same thing is happening today. Still, all of hell is combining with human forces to crush the life of Christ on earth. The life of Christ today is in his Church, in his Body, and the devil is using many different methods to kill it. In one part of the world he is using revolution and persecution; in another part of the world he is using affluence to kill the life of Christ. I have made the statement, "It could well be that capitalism has killed more Christians than communism has." I refer, of course, to spiritual life, not to physical life. It doesn't matter how many people may be killed physically by the devil; that in itself does not kill the Church of Christ. But prosperity and wealth and materialism kill the spiritual life of Christians, and they fail to multiply. That is what kills the Church, and with it the possibility of passing on the life of Christ to more and more people around the world.

I love the United States and its warm-hearted, generous

67

people, but I have to say that America is an excellent illustration of what I am saying. I am convinced that what we are seeing in the U.S. at the moment has more to do with Christian culture than with Jesus Christ. If most of the people have a true vital relationship with Jesus Christ, how is it that there is so much violent crime, immorality, and occultism in the land? Where is the influence of the Church?

I am an avid reader of the *U.S. News and World Report* and each year the magazine asks, "What institutions in America have the most influence in the life of the nation?" They list thirty that wield the most power in leading America in a certain direction. The two institutions I would have thought would have had the most influence in a nation which now claims that two-thirds of its adult population are born again are "religion" and the "family." Yet the amazing thing is that, in the 1979 report, "family" comes in 26th and religion 28th. According to this poll, these two pillars of the nation are virtually without influence in guiding the nation. This is, to me, absolutely shattering. It just baffles me to see it, yet my only conclusion is that America is a materialistic society with a Christian varnish that makes it self-indulgent and therefore powerless to make real changes. I make the same observation also for all of the so-called Christian nations of Western Europe.

That is why I say that we must be careful that we don't export Western Christianity, which is the accusation that comes to us now, particularly from the Latin American countries.

The persecuted Church is totally different from that in capitalistic countries. In it we see a resurgence of the faith, yet without the prestige that many in the evangelical movement on the outside seek; it is often without priests and pastors; certainly without public buildings; but yet it is a powerful, brave, and influential Church. It is so influential that atheistic authorities keep trying to wipe it out. They are so scared ot it.

But back in Nehemiah's day, Jerusalem had been destroyed, and the devil wanted to keep it that way because Jerusalem was destined to play a vital role in the life of Jesus Christ and his crucifixion. That is why the ministry of Nehemiah was so vital for the kingdom of God. Nehemiah was not just a man who was going to rebuild the walls and gates of Jerusalem; Nehemiah was a part of that tremendous plan of God for the redemption of the whole world. His work may seem mundane— he is just building a wall—yet it is deeply spiritual.

As we go out into the world to evangelize, we don't just go to win a few souls for Christ here and there. We are a part of that great plan that God has for the world, a plan which comes both in the fullness of time and in the fullness of the number of those who are to be saved. Since, as we faithfully serve our living God, we take part in that great plan of God, we need to think and talk about strategy and strategic planning.

Many people want to know if we, in Open Doors, have a blueprint, a strategy, for our work. Yes, we do, but first of all I have to explain that most people have a wrong concept of our ministry. They believe that we are exclusively Bible smugglers. But that is not so, although I have to agree that that is the most spectacular aspect of what we do, and that certainly captures the imagination of many. They like to hear of our cloak-and-dagger operations, of our derring-do couriers.

But really our main thrust is the total care of the suffering Church, and that includes the ministry of encouragement, physical help, and instruction as well as distributing Bibles, Christian literature, and hymn books. Unless our ministry to the suffering Church is well-rounded, we miss the point. This is what I would call our strategy and why research is such an important factor in this.

Before our Open Doors courier teams go on a trip, we invest in a tremendous amount of research, something we consider absolutely vital. A research team is sent to discover the real needs of the believers inside; this happens in Russia, China, Africa, and across Eastern Europe. Our researchers bring back what I call a shopping list of what we need to take back to help and build up the Body on the inside.

That is why I think that the tourist going in with Bibles is of limited use. Of course he can place a couple of Scriptures on a bench of a church, but really there needs to be a professional approach to the problem, because it exists on such a huge scale.

Let's return to the steps that led Nehemiah in developing his strategic planning. Three things happened within three days. Through his honest inquiries he got to know the needs of his fellow Jews and Jerusalem. He has the spiritual experience of humbling himself before God and making confession of sins. As a result of these two things, he reaches the point at which he is willing to give up all his privileges and rights.

These steps have to do with a whole city that has to be rebuilt, with a whole nation that has to be regathered. Nehemiah, of course, cannot do that alone. But when God calls a leader, he never calls him to work alone. God always gives followers to a leader. Before Nehemiah begins to recruit people to work with him, he does something else first.

In chapter 2, verse 11, we see that he has already been in Jerusalem for three days. There was not much of Jerusalem left: no big houses or palaces, no walls or gates. Nehemiah now reports (verses 12 and 13), "Then I arose in the night, I and a few men with me; and I told no one what my God had put into my heart to do for Jerusalem. There was no beast with me but the beast which I rode. I went out by night by the Valley Gate to the Jackal's Well and to the Dung Gate, and I inspected the walls of Jerusalem which were broken down and its gates which had been destroyed by fire."

Note verse 16: "And the officials did not know where I had gone or what I was doing; and I had not yet told the Jews, the priests, the nobles, the officials, and the rest that were to do the work." The whole thing was still in his own heart and in his own mind. He was still all by himself, bringing the problem to his God, but he had the courage to go out himself and inspect the ruins personally. Now that's the fourth point that I want to mention about Nehemiah.

At first he only hears about the need. Now I could tell you much about the need in many countries of the world, enough for you to begin to pray intelligently about it. Maybe even enough to begin an argument with somebody who says this is not so. But it is a different thing if you would go there personally and see with your own eyes whether or not these things are the way Brother Andrew told you they are. That's why I believe in people traveling to other countries to find out facts for themselves. Don't just base your opinion on what other people have seen and report to you, because it may be only part of the truth, and reporting part of the truth may be worse than telling a lie.

I think we should go there ourselves and see. Go with an open mind, maybe without telling other people about it, just as Nehemiah did there that night. He did not tell anybody, not even those who were going to work with him. I think that is a statement of faith.

Nehemiah was the only one who knew that they were going to do the work. Now that's really a trip! That's the eye of faith. He had a vision; God gave him the vision. God knows that you are going to do it, even if you still don't know it.

Now the stage is set to begin recruiting, and I want to draw your attention to three words in the passage in chapter 2, starting at verse 17: "Then I said to them, 'You see the trouble we are in, how Jerusalem lies in ruins with its gates burned. *Come,* let us build the wall of Jerusalem, that we may no longer suffer disgrace.' And I told them of the hand of my God which had been upon me for good, and also of the words which the king had spoken to me. And they said, 'Let us *rise* up and *build.*' So they strengthened their hands for the good work."

Now here are the three words: come, rise, build.

Come! That is the recruiting cry. Why does a leader say it? Because he has a vision; because he knows there is a ministry to be done; because he knows the will of God is leading him; because he also knows that he cannot do it alone. Leaders need people to *come* with them.

The second word, *rise,* suggests that the workers must prepare for the task that lies before them. Preparation will involve the same points that we have just discussed in the life of Nehemiah. You must know the need. You must humble yourself before God and confess your sins. You have to be ready to give up your job, your rights, and your privileges. You must go and see for yourself how big the need is: in other words, go out into the streets, go out into the highways and byways of sin, as Jesus told us to do.

When I was in Bible school in Glasgow, Scotland, God gave

me a little mission field. It was the slums of Glasgow. I don't think there were any worse slums in all of Europe than those in Glasgow. The area called Patrick was so dangerous that even the policemen were not allowed to go in alone. People were being murdered almost every day; it was an extremely dangerous area. God just laid it on my heart that that was where I had to witness for Jesus Christ.

I would go into those dark, dank, depressing housing areas where all the light bulbs had been broken or stolen. On every corner was a shabby pub where men would get drunk on whisky, and wives would cry because there was no money left for food or clothing. I would go into these dirty Dickensian hostelries to try and talk with some of the men and also give out tracts. I always asked permission from the pub's proprietor. They never refused because I am sure they had consciences about what they were doing.

In one smoke-filled bar I met Jock Kearney, a hard-drinking Scotsman with whom I struck up an immediate conversation.

"Come and see me tomorrow at my place, laddie," he slurred as he stumbled out clasping a tract that I had given him.

I invited Albert, a fellow student from the WEC college, to come with me to see Jock. Full of trepidation, we picked our way along the threatening streets and up the pitch-black staircase to his fourth-floor apartment. As we climbed upwards we tripped over all sorts of garbage that had been left rotting on the stairs. Jock blinked as he saw us at the door.

"Come in," he said. When we got inside that darkened room which was lit by one naked bulb, we were horrified to see the state of the room. Wallpaper peeled from the wall, paint peeled from the ceiling, and the sink was full of unwashed cups and plates.

I had hoped that by now he would have sobered up, but he was as drunk as ever. Suddenly, he urinated in the sink.

"I'll fix you a cup of tea," he then told us, picking up a couple of the unwashed cups from that sink. My stomach turned, but I knew I couldn't refuse.

"Lord, please help me not to be sick," I prayed as I was handed the nauseous brew.

As we talked, Jock turned his rough unshaven face towards

me, and said, "Hey Dutchman, you used to be in the army. What's the law of war?"

I thought for a moment, and then replied, "It's your life or mine. That's the law of war."

"Right . . ." he said. "Too right."

I sat transfixed as he went over to a drawer, opened it, and pulled out a big cut-throat razor. Slowly, deliberately, he unsheathed it and came for me.

By now, as he spoke, his eyes rolled ominously. "I'm going to kill you," he suddenly screamed. I felt the razor at my throat. A petrified Albert stayed in his seat. He prayed like he had never done before.

As Jock held the razor at my throat, I managed to gasp out, "Yes Jock, it is my life or yours, and because of that you can't do this. Someone has already died to save both your life and mine.

"His name is Jesus Christ."

I quickly continued. "Look, Jock, Jesus came into the world because of these laws of war and because of the spiritual warfare where only one can win and another must lose.

"One has to die so the other will live. That's exactly what Jesus Christ did."

Jock still held the knife so it just nicked the skin of my throat, so I kept talking about how Jesus had shed his blood that we both might live, and the forgiveness that he offered.

"He died so you might live, Jock."

Slowly, but surely, he withdrew the rusty razor and stepped back and looked at me with utter disbelief. He couldn't believe what I had told him. Then he folded it away and put it in the cupboard.

Feeling that maybe I shouldn't take the matter any further, I said breathlessly, "Jock, that is just fine. Thank you for putting the razor away. We will leave now, but we'll come back to speak more about Jesus."

Albert and I almost ran out of the place. We were ashen-faced and shaken, but grateful to the Lord that it hadn't been any worse.

I decided that I shouldn't take Albert with me on my next visit. I was afraid that if the same happened again, Albert might not be able to constrain himself and would try to intervene. This, I was sure, would certainly guarantee my bloody death. So I went alone.

Still disheveled, but thankfully not drunk, Jock answered the door and invited me in.

"I'm so sorry about the other night. It was a terrible thing I did to you," he said shamefacedly. "It's the drink, you know. It makes me do terrible things."

I told him it was all right. I understood.

"Jesus still loves you Jock. Why don't you just pray and ask him into your life? He can change all of this."

Jock suddenly sank to his knees and in a childlike manner poured out his heart to Jesus, asking him to forgive him and accept him just as he was. "I'm a rotten person Jesus, but I want to follow you—if you'll have me," he prayed.

Jesus did, and his life was transformed there and then. It was an incredible moment for both of us. Now you may read about terrible situations in other big cities like New York, Amsterdam, Calcutta, or Jakarta, and you may cry when you read about them. You may have a burden on your heart to pray for those poor people, but it's quite different to go there yourself to see people lying on the pavement, in desperate situations in those slums. You have to know firsthand what the situation is; it's part of training. There you will be faced with the question, "Am I capable of communicating the love of God to these people?" You must face that question; it is part of your preparation.

Another part of your preparation is Bible study. It's a marvelous privilege if God lets you go to a school of evangelism or a Bible school.

I believe it is a great advantage to learn how to study the Bible; to discover how to work with other people, and live with them as well. You rub shoulders at a Bible school for two or three years with a variety of others. They come from different denominational backgrounds. You learn to pray together and go out and witness as teams.

That's why I advocate an organization such as Operation Mobilization. On a ship for a year. I tell you, you certainly get to know yourself in that time.

I have to admit, however, that I was not a very good student.

I was too involved in my outreach work and my health suffered badly. I was generally exhausted most of the time and also had a painful slipped disc.

When the time came for graduation, I went to see Stewart Dinnen, the director of studies, and asked him if I could *not* be awarded a diploma.

He turned to me with a look that said, "Andrew, you must be crazy." Being British, however, he didn't voice that comment.

"You see, sir, I don't want any mission society to take me into service just because I have a diploma from a Bible school. I want to follow the Lord and only do his will."

"I want to have God's approval. If not I will go back to work as an economist."

"If that's what you want, Andrew, that's great," he said. "That will save me three minutes of writing it out."

I was the first student to leave that school without a diploma.

Now are you ready to rise above the circumstances, diploma or no diploma? *Rise* until you know that you are in touch with heaven itself?

I spend much of my time flying in jets and each time I take off I see the power of those engines overcome a law that has defeated man for countless centuries—the law of gravity. When those engines are switched on and we zoom down a runway, we suddenly rise above the clouds. You have the greatest power in the universe in you if you are a believer—the Holy Spirit.

Rise up and be free!

I was in Brazil recently, and there a leftist politician told me that the Pentecostal movement there has elevated these people above their circumstances. They have risen from poverty, not to riches, but a level higher.

Now you should rise until you know that your message comes from God's holy place and not from books. I pray that you will be a man or a woman of one book—God's Book.

Now you are ready to build.

PART TWO
BUILD

EIGHT
DOES PRAYER
CHANGE THINGS—
OR US?

A basic problem of people everywhere is the need of a foundation. When the friends of Nehemiah told him the walls of Jerusalem had been destroyed and the gates burned by fire, they were really saying that they had lost their foundation, and life as they knew it was no longer possible.

There is a very interesting verse in Psalm 11, verse 3: "If the foundations are destroyed, what can the righteous do?" You can apply that verse to the society in which you live: if the foundations of God are destroyed in your nation through permissiveness or through immorality or through revolution, if the family is broken up through divorce or by government decree, if the foundations are being destroyed, there is nothing that even a righteous man can do. So the need to lay a foundation is the first need that we want to identify.

What is the foundation? I turn to 1 Corinthians, chapter 3, verse 11: "For no other foundation can anyone lay than that which is laid, which is Jesus Christ." Ephesians chapter 2, verse 20 says further that the household of God is built upon the foundation of the apostles and prophets, Christ Jesus himself being the cornerstone. These verses do not contradict each other; the only message all the apostles and prophets preached was Christ Jesus as the foundation.

There must be a foundation. Without a foundation, you cannot build. To repeat Psalm 11, verse 3: "If the foundations are destroyed, what can the righteous do?" And the answer is implied in that question: there is nothing the righteous can do if there is no foundation.

There must be a foundation in our own lives. All that we do in our lives—all that we do not do—must be firmly based upon that one foundation, Jesus Christ. Nothing lasting can be built except upon that one foundation. No lasting peace can result if it is not founded on Jesus Christ. No lasting relationship with people can be built unless based upon that one foundation— whether a marriage, or a friendship, or a church fellowship, or even a business. If it is to have lasting results for the kingdom of God, it must be built on that one foundation.

I want to ask you, is Jesus Christ the foundation of your life? Or is your faith still based on tradition, even if that is Christian tradition? Or is your faith based on the faith of your parents? Remember, we speak about God's children, and God has no grandchildren. We must know that our lives are based on the foundation—Jesus Christ! Once your foundation has been laid by personal faith in Jesus Christ, then you can begin to build, or maybe to rebuild, your life of service. Let it be only on that foundation.

We also need a divine protection in our lives, and God wants to build on that foundation a wall of protection through his people. God himself has laid the foundation. And now he calls us to build.

When Nehemiah's friends told him that the walls were broken down and the gates burned by fire, it meant that there was no protection for the people who lived there. No person in this world can live without protection, whether he is a believer or an unbeliever.

Now God has provided enough protection for every individual who was ever born and who is alive today. But not everybody accepts that protection, and of course most people don't know such protection is available. That is why there are so many personal tragedies in the world.

We as Christians must be on our guard to make sure our protection is there, because the devil will always try to attack. He will try to attack you in your mind, and you know that if he can influence your way of thinking, he can eventually destroy your entire life. If he cannot get at your mind when you are awake, he will try when you are asleep. You know you can have terribly bad dreams. Now, who is protecting you when you sleep? That is why, before you go to sleep, you speak to the Lord. You claim his protection on your entire being while you are asleep. And, probably, somebody else in the world is praying for you while you are asleep.

Now you know why people working for the Lord must make sure believers all over the world are praying for them. There is tremendous value in intercession. If at any time of day or night God prompts you to pray for a person, you had better do it at that moment because that may be a moment when that particular person is under special satanic attack. God wants to use your prayers to give extra protection to that person.

This principle came into action when one of our teams was caught in Bulgaria with a load of Scriptures. The team, which consisted of a Dutch doctor and a pastor, was interrogated for many hours and then locked up. The pastor was thrown into prison, while the doctor—a diabetic—was taken to a hotel room and a guard was posted outside.

The authorities, however, made one mistake. They forgot there was a phone in the room, and so at three in the morning the doctor phoned me. "Andrew," he whispered, hoping the watchdog wouldn't hear what he said, "we've been caught and they have locked the pastor up and taken all our Bibles. We could be sent to prison for six years if we are found guilty. Please pray and get the whole 'family' praying . . . please."

With that the line went dead. I quickly called up our prayer groups around the world, and soon hundreds were on their knees for the trapped team in Bulgaria.

The Lord impressed me to make contact with a friendly embassy, and despite the early hour they began delicate negotiations with the Bulgarians for the release of the men.

Corry and I quickly dressed and we drove to visit the nearby families of the doctor and the pastor. At both homes, we sat and held hands and prayed that the Lord would solve this problem. I had a deep peace about the whole matter because I knew so many people were praying. Three days later they were out and back in Holland. There had been no trial and, except for having to pay a fine and losing their car and the load of Bibles, they were free. It was a terrific deliverance.

Whenever something like this happens, we don't believe that our personnel have to go to prison, because we have other power available—the power of prayer. That's why we at Open Doors stress the importance of the prayer groups and their ministry.

The Bible tells us that when Satan fell out of heaven, he pulled with him one-third of the angelic powers. So one-third of all the former angels are now demons. Demons don't die and they don't wear out. They are as much alive and active as the angels of God are, and unless God protects a man, he will be the prey of those demons. Paul says, in 1 Timothy chapter 4, verse 10, that God "is the Savior of all men, especially of those who believe." In other words, even unbelievers have been protected by the Almighty God, because if God would not protect unbelieving people, they would all become demon-possessed. Some people are demon-possessed, because for some reason or other their protection has been taken away and they have become an easy prey of the devil.

God protects our people. God even protects nations. I am a strong believer in God's protection on specific nations. For instance, he has a special divine protection on Israel. Humanly speaking, Israel should have been wiped off the map many times, but God has his hand on that nation. They are not Christians, and there is less religious liberty in Israel than there is in the Soviet Union. It's very hard to evangelize in Israel; it is actually easier to preach the gospel in Russia. The moment you begin to approach Jews and tell them about Jesus Christ, you are in trouble in Israel. But Israel is God's people, even if they do not believe in their Messiah. In addition, God has a future plan for Israel and therefore is protecting that country in a very specific way.

I also believe that God has his hand especially on the United States of America, because in America there is all the potential for world evangelism, and world evangelism is God's primary purpose. God will protect any nation in which he sees the potential for world evangelism. I don't have to agree with America's policies and I don't have to agree with its president or its way of capitalism, but I have to learn to look at that country the way God looks at it. God sees in a country the potential for world evangelism, and therefore God will protect that nation.

Nehemiah realized that people cannot live without protection, but a wall is not the only kind of protection needed. In chapter 4, verse 14, Nehemiah encourages his friends: "Do not be afraid of them. Remember the Lord, who is great and terrible, and fight for your brethren, your sons, your daughters, your wives, and your homes."

The enemy's sole purpose is to take away the arm of protection that God has given us. The enemy reminds us that we are without protection. But God is the greatest psychologist in the world. God never tells us to do something in our own strength. Before Jesus told his disciples that they must go out into all the world and preach the gospel, he first said, "I have all authority in heaven and on earth, therefore go ye into all the world." God first gives us enough encouragement so that we can then obey whatever he tells us to do.

Now that is exactly what Nehemiah is doing. Why is the protection taken away from his people? It has been an act of the enemy. Nehemiah first says, "Don't be afraid of them." That is not an easy statement for the people. They have been robbed by the enemy; their defense system has been taken away from them; there is not more protection for them and they are so afraid.

But then Nehemiah encourages and strengthens them in the Lord. He says, "Remember the Lord, who is great and terrible." Think of the greatness of our God. Remember, when you enter the battle, one man with God is a majority.

I have stood in the Red Squares of many Communist cities and I have watched millions of people parading. I have watched them in Havana, in Peking, in Bucharest, in Budapest, in Prague, in East Berlin, and in Moscow. I have watched as they carried the red banner; I have heard their revolutionary songs; I have seen the determination on young faces; and I knew they intended to conquer the whole world.

In most of those places I was alone. I was just standing there with the precious little Book. I pressed it to my heart and the Book spoke to my heart. What did the Book say? "Every knee shall bow and every tongue shall confess that Jesus Christ is Lord." It made me feel good because I knew that Jesus and I were the majority. There was no need for me to be afraid. All I had to do was obey his orders.

Finally, Nehemiah charged the people, "Fight for your brethren!" Nehemiah was concerned about their brethren in Jerusalem. Today I say we should be concerned about our brethren in the Communist countries, our brethren in Africa, our brethren in other areas of revolution and turmoil. We must fight for our brethren.

Do you know why the Communists despise Christians? It's not just because they are against religion, but they also despise us because we make no active effort to evangelize Communist countries.

A leading Czech Communist once said, "I can only honor my opponent in a debate if he makes an all-out effort to convert me." This is a typical Communist attitude. The fact that we are afraid of them makes them despise us. They want to fight. They are not that convinced that they are right, but since we don't challenge their constant lies, they—and we—eventually accept them as truth. They are waiting for anyone to challenge them, because an honest Communist is an idealist. It is marvelous to meet someone who is an idealist, whatever his persuasion. It's deadening to meet a Christian who is not going to stand up for his faith.

Why do the Arab nations so despise us now? It's because we have made no attempt to claim any rights for Western people when they impose their restrictions on us. If we would stand up for the Christians in their countries, they would respect us. Power always despises weakness. If we really made an all-out effort to evangelize Eastern Europe or even Russia itself, they would respect us. But at the moment we mostly stand by, helpless and frightened, and say, "It can't be done."

The Communists are very active in infiltrating our society, but we do very little to infiltrate their society. So they figure that if our religion is not good enough for the whole world, if it is not even good enough for the capitalist part of the world, then they will destroy that religion. Maybe they are right!

But the message of Jesus Christ is for the whole world! If we do not fight for our brethren, if we do not stand up and speak up for those who are being oppressed, if we make no personal sacrifices to reach the unreached, then our religion is not true Christianity. We might as well have revolution. That revolution will destroy our churches; it will destroy our religion and our Christianity.

But somewhere, some people will survive with a little Book and in that Book they will find Jesus Christ. They may then develop a form of Christianity that bears no resemblance to what we call Christianity. They will probably never build a church building.

The earlier believers were not concerned with church buildings. They came together in the homes and in the fields, but they stirred all of Asia Minor and Greece. Paul says the faith of those groups of believers was spread all over that area. It may well be that God will let the revolution come over our countries to destroy the manmade gods and to destroy the manmade religion we call Christianity.

The only true Christianity is to take the love of God to every person in the world. "Fight for your brethren" is a divine command.

Remember the sequence Nehemiah used in verse 14. After "fight for your brethren," he adds, "and for your sons, your daughters, your wives, and your homes." Our first reaction to that verse might be that there is something wrong with the order. Surely, as a Christian, I must first provide protection for my own family, and then second, for my brethren. Why does this verse first say "your brethren" and then "for your sons, your daughters, your wives and your homes"? Has God made a mistake?

The Almighty God knows that if you take care of your brethren first, then you will never neglect your sons, daughters, wives, and your homes. If we cannot love those who are outside the kingdom of God, it means that we have not allowed the love of God to come into our hearts. If the love of God is not in our hearts, then we are not going to do much for our own family. Many Christian families are breaking up because they have not allowed the love of God to rule in their hearts. That's one of the opportunities for the devil to destroy the Church.

Let me sound one note of caution. Some time ago a survey of

Christians was taken in the United States. The question was, "What, in your opinion, is the biggest mission field in the world today?"

The amazing answer was this: "North America." Here is the danger: if Christians, wherever they are found, think that their place is the most important mission field in the world, then they will have no outreach to the rest of the world. If they think their highest calling is to protect what they have, then they will lose all they have. Jesus said, "If you want to keep your life, you will lose it, but if you are willing to lose your life, you will keep it."

If I, as a Dutch Christian, and you in whatever country you live, would have as our highest concern to build a wall about our own families in order to protect them from, say, the revolution, that is the quickest way to lose our families. Because then the evil powers will go unchecked and unchallenged, and the atheistic God-hating forces will grow stronger. They are not going to stop at that little wall that I have built personally around my little family. The best way to protect what God has given me is to go to those who present themselves as our enemies and win them for Christ!

Early in 1980 I was in war-torn El Salvador in Central America. There I had a secret meeting with leftist guerrillas who were holding the South African ambassador, Archibald Dunn. They were surprised when I put to them my request to see their prisoner.

"Why do you want to see him?" asked their grim-faced leader, who claimed to be a Christian. I replied, "The reason is that I also belong to a liberation movement and since I am on a par with you, I think I can ask to see him."

The leader was a little surprised that someone like me could claim to be part of a liberation movement, especially as I didn't carry a gun. So I explained that my leader, Jesus Christ, was the greatest liberator of men of all time.

He then questioned my motive and claimed that the ambassador was an "exploiter" and was being punished for this. "You have no right to punish anybody," I said firmly. "Judgment belongs to God. It is not your job to punish anybody from another country for a crime that he may have committed against black people in South Africa."

The leader protested and claimed to have a letter from the black people of South Africa "to punish him."

They turned down my request but still I felt the Lord had allowed me to go into the "enemy camp" to talk to them about Christ. Later I heard they had murdered the ambassador because a ransom had not been paid for him.

Our only chance to win the Communist nations for Christ is to go in to them. It's the same with the world at large: we need to bring the Good News to the places where people are. We should be witnessing in the bars, the gambling casinos, the sports stadiums, the market place. We need to infiltrate these places, not as secret agents, but we need to show our colors from the start. People will respect us for coming to them.

Sadly, evangelism, for many, is to hold a meeting in a hall and expect the people to come in to hear. But Jesus said, "I will make you fishers of men." It's like going on to a beach and erecting two large poles with a cross on top and a net in between the two poles. We then expect the fish to jump out of the water into our net—and then we wonder why our net is not filled. That's not the way to catch fish. We've got to go where the fish are; we've got to let down our nets and catch them.

Why is it that one of the strongest churches in the world is in Siberia? It is because the real believers from Russia who were deported there, even before the 1917 revolution, couldn't keep their mouths shut. They won many others for Christ.

In case I sound negative about the value of a God-centered home, let me remind you of the high value God has placed on the home. It is a wonderful thing—the home. Some of you may not know much of the blessing of a Christian home. If it functions well, it is a piece of heaven on earth. But often it is a representation of hell on earth.

In 1949, when I was seeking God, I felt terribly lonely. I missed my mother so much, because she had died while I was out in the Far East; she was such a saint. My brothers and sisters were getting married, and I still had not found peace in Jesus Christ. I felt so terribly lonely because I felt I had no home any more. Then God opened the Bible to me and I found a verse that spoke to my soul: Psalm 68, verse 6, "God gives the desolate a home to dwell in." He places the lonely people in a home to live in!

I was desolate and lonely and God said, "I will place you in a home. . . ." I think if anything at all drew me into the kingdom of God, it must have been this thought. I wasn't that much under conviction of sin. Oh, I was a terrible sinner! But I had an intense longing to live in a home—not just in a house, but in a home. And that pulled me into the kingdom of God. So let us build homes together within the protection of God.

Now let us look at another aspect of protection. In Numbers chapter 14, verse 9, is recorded one of those moments of confrontation between the nation of Israel on one side and Moses and Aaron on the other. It is after the first espionage trip into the Promised Land. The majority of the spies had only reported on the physical realities of what faced them. They were very problem-conscious and came out with a negative report. But there were also Caleb and Joshua—men of God. They saw with spiritual eyes; they saw what God could do. They believed in the supernatural and they saw the potential if the people of Israel would move on with their God. They remembered that God had said, "I have given you the land." Because of that Word of God, they made a profession of faith. The majority of the spies either did not remember the Word of God, or perhaps they knew what God had said, but they thought, "Yes, but we still have to conquer it."

Joshua and Caleb responded in faith. They spoke to all the people: "Only do not rebel against the Lord; and do not fear the people of the land, for they are bread for us; their protection is removed from them, and the Lord is with us; do not fear them."

I want to note only one aspect of this very wonderful and strange verse, and that is the reference to protection. Even heathen nations have protection. The devil can protect a group of people so that the Word of God cannot get through to them.

I see a very strong illustration of this in the Muslim world. The Muslim world is the only bloc in the world that has not yet been penetrated effectively with the gospel. The Muslim world is strongly in the grip of the false prophet. There is no false religion that comes so close to the biblical concept of the kingdom of God. When you read their holy book, the Koran, you find many of the same stories that you find in the Bible. Even Jesus Christ is mentioned often, and counted among the main prophets of the Muslim religion. I see a demonic form of protection around the Muslim world, and there just hasn't been enough prayer and sacrifice yet to break through that devilish protection.

Don't forget that until 1945, seven-eighths of the entire Arab world was colonized by so-called Christian nations. But they did not encourage gospel preaching because they did not want to antagonize the Arab people; they only wanted to exploit those nations. Now the Arabs are presenting us with the bill; we have to pay more for their oil.

The moment that the oil crisis began, God gave me a vision. I have never complained about the higher oil prices, because I saw that billions of dollars would flow into the Arab countries and they would have to spend that money somewhere. They couldn't possibly spend it all in their own countries, so they would have to spend it in the Western world. They would have to buy technology from us, and that technology would have to be accompanied by Western technicians. I could see openings coming in their "protection." Many Christians are now going in as technicians and specialists and teachers to reach the Arab people with the love of God.

But let's go back to Numbers 14. What protection did those heathen nations in Canaan have? From studies of the history of that time and area, we understand that those nations in Canaan were the most immoral on the face of the earth. They were absolutely the worst possible people in the world. That's why God had decided to destroy them. But because they were so much the property of the devil, the devil had a special system of protection around them and there was only one way of breaking through that defense system. Only the people of God could do it, and God announced to his people, "Don't be afraid, for their protection has been taken away from them."

Today, as we pray for the Muslim countries, how shall we pray? That their demonic system of protection will be broken down? Only then can we reach them with the message of the love of God.

But let's also apply this same principle to individuals we pray for. Why does it seem that some people are simply unreachable? Is it because God doesn't love them? Why can we not reach them? Because there is a devilish system of protection around them, and by prayer and fasting we can break through that system.

So there are two systems of protection. I hope that all of you are very much aware of God's system of protection—that wall of divine protection not only around your individual life, but around the family of which you are a part, around your particular home church as a family of God's children, and around your country as one of the nations that God has blessed so much.

NINE
HOW TO RESPOND
TO PRESSURE

Whenever you are doing a work for God, you are going to meet
with opposition. If you have no opposition to your ministry,
then I think you should begin to feel uneasy. If the devil is not
after you, then you ought to worry that maybe you're not
doing anything.

In the case of Nehemiah, he and his people were doing a
great work. They faced a tremendous challenge, but God had
encouraged them. God worked in their hearts to make them
willing to serve sacrificially. Nothing great will ever happen
without sacrificial service. To work in the kingdom will
always cost you something, and the more it costs you, the
more results you will have, if you work with great faith and
enthusiasm.

Opposition came early to Nehemiah. We read about a few
people who were against Nehemiah from the very start. It
says in chapter 2, verse 10, that "it displeased them [Sanballat
and Tobiah] greatly that some one had come to seek the
welfare of the children of Israel."

The enemy of souls cannot stand for anyone to seek the
welfare of the people. The devil is the enemy of souls, so
anyone seeking the salvation of souls becomes a target for
the devil. This is always the basic reason for opposition.

Opposition comes in several forms. In the first stages of
Nehemiah's work for Jerusalem, in chapter 2, verse 19, it says,

"But when Sanballat the Horonite and Tobiah the servant, the Ammonite, and Geshem the Arab heard of it, they derided us and despised us." The very first thing that will happen, even before you start to work for the Lord, is that people will begin to ridicule you. They will try to make a fool of you. "You are crazy to give up your job." "What good do you think you can do in the world?" "You are not a gifted person; there is nothing you can do to change the world!" "You're just a religious fanatic."

They not only ridicule you, they seem to despise you and say terrible things against you. In Nehemiah's case they said, "What is this thing that you do? Are you rebelling against the king?" This is the beginning of a whole campaign of talking against the ones who are going to do something good for Jerusalem.

We find more ridicule in chapter 4, verse 2, "And he [Sanballat] said in the presence of his brethren and of the army of Samaria, 'What are these feeble Jews doing? Will they restore things? Will they sacrifice? Will they finish up in a day? Will they revive the stones out of the heaps of rubbish, and burned ones at that?'"

Do you see how terribly negative this ridicule was? They were not just talking against what these Jews were doing; they were also calling them "feeble Jews." These people, men like Nehemiah, who had traveled over long distances, were not weak, thin, poor-looking beggars. If they could finish half the wall in a few weeks, they were obviously fit for work. So the enemy just wanted to make them look ridiculous.

Never listen to people who downgrade other people. It's the devil's trick. He is the accuser of the brethren. Man is made in the image of God. Man is beautiful and strong. Only the devil says, "Man is nothing."

I want you to love other people, and I want you to love yourself, because God loves you. You should never despise anyone that God loves; if God loves you, you should love you. Remember that all the potential of the life of Jesus Christ is in you and me. When you realize that fact, your Christian life can be one of fun, joy, and total relaxation. Don't ever downgrade yourself. God loves the whole world, and you're part of it.

Sanballat presented a whole list of negatives. "Will they

restore things?" What is he talking about, since the Jews are only rebuilding the wall? "Will they sacrifice?" No one has even mentioned the temple yet. "Will they finish up in one day?" Of course not, they will take a long time to finish the whole thing.

He even asked if they would bring back to life the stones that were burned with fire. I'm told that they used a sandstone which, if it became very hot, as when the city was burned, it would just crumble and become dust. When later the Romans destroyed Jerusalem, in A.D. 70, they simply started a big fire at the bottom of the wall, and the large stones crumbled and fell. Remember Jesus said that "not one stone shall be left on top of the other." Nehemiah's enemy had a real point, I suppose, when he asked, "Are they going to make real live stones again of the ashes?"

Of course, when somebody starts to make funny remarks about a situation like that, then others want to make even funnier comments. So, in verse 3, Tobiah, the Ammonite, says, "Yes, what they are building—if a fox goes up on it he will break down their stone wall!"

They are really making the thing look foolish! I tell you that whenever you begin to work as a Christian, other people will say, "You are crazy! Listen, if your government and your political party and your big church and your missions cannot change it, how can you change it?" Many men and women of God have been put off by the attack of ridicule. Have you recognized that in your own life?

How do we answer that one? The only right answer is the answer that Nehemiah gave. He does not talk to them, he talks to God. Look at verse 4. His immediate reaction is, "Hear, O our God, for we are despised; turn back their taunt upon their own heads, and give them up to be plundered in a land where they are captives."

He prays. He even suggests to the Almighty God how punishment should come to his tormentors. What an insight Nehemiah has into the reality of prayer. He knows what prayer really is. Prayer is laying hold of God; it is speaking to God about people. Prayer is both for the blessing of certain people and restraining the action of other people.

Nehemiah has learned to pray against situations. This is

something we have to learn. Pray against the enemy! Pray against an unhealthy development in society.

By prayer we move the arms of God, so in prayer we must learn to be more aggressive. We should not just *ask*, but *act* in prayer. In other words, tell God what to do.

Do you think that is dangerous? It all depends on how well we know God, or how much we understand the principles of the kingdom. Unless we rise above the level on which the devil can constantly defeat us, we will never learn how to reign with Christ in heaven.

I do not say you should ever expect to arrive at a level at which you are immune to attack. If you are not attacked, you are not doing anything. But the outcome of the attack depends on your reaction, not on the fierceness of the attack. If your reaction is to bring the problem, right then and there, to God, then God will take care of it.

You don't have to defend yourself. You do not have to defend your cause. You do not even have to defend the Bible or to defend God. Just do the job that God has given you to do.

Now that is the first attack that is mounted—the attack of ridicule—but because Nehemiah and his friends are not turned away by it, their enemies become angrier. In chapter 4, verse 7, it records that when the enemies heard that the repairing of the wall was continuing under the blessing of God, they were very angry. Oh, yes, the opposition can stiffen! Once they realized they could not win with words of ridicule, they all plotted together to cause confusion in Jerusalem (verse 8). They see that their words of ridicule had not had the effect they had hoped they would, so they plot something more drastic: "We'll have to create confusion in their camp."

If the devil can give us a wrong concept about the real battle, then he has won it. Oh, the confusion in Christianity today! We confuse nationalistic issues with the kingdom of God. We confuse race issues with the things of the Church. This is a strategy of the devil.

Nehemiah knew about this new plan. What is his reaction? In the very next verse he recounts, "And we prayed to our God, and set a guard as a protection against them day and night."

It is the spiritual reaction of God's workers that gives them the victory. The answer is "watch and pray"—only in this case it is "pray and watch." Unless we consciously protect our spirit against the attacks of the enemy, we will become an easy prey. Immediately bring the conflict to God.

In verse 11, there is a third attack plan, a very deadly one. The enemies say, "They will not know or see till we come into the midst of them and kill them and stop the work."

Personally, I find this attack the easiest to deal with. It is the most primitive one. It is the way in which they have fought wars in centuries past. This is the classic pattern of the persecution of the Church. Just kill them and then you've won the battle.

Uganda is the most recent illustration of this. The holocaust against the believers began when Idi Amin became friends with Colonel Muammar Gadhafi of Libya and King Faisal of Saudi Arabia. The president's fever for the Moslem faith reached its height during the visit of the Arab king to Kampala. Faisal brought with him royal gifts, including an enormous platter of gold and a golden sword. He told the impressed Amin: "With this sword, Moslemize your country."

Amin decided to set up an Islamic republic in Uganda and told his Moslem friends that he needed some cash to do this. Both Libya and Saudi Arabia fell for Amin's lies and gave generous donations to the Jihad (holy war) Fund, to be used, in the words of a visiting Libyan diplomat, "to eliminate the few remaining Christians and turn Uganda into a Moslem state."

Eventually, after Amin had personally murdered Janani Luwum, the beloved Archbishop of Uganda, the killings of Christians reached an unprecedented scale. Out of the estimated 500,000 people murdered in Uganda by Amin's terror machine during his eight years of misrule, a large proportion were Christians.

But still Amin wasn't able to wipe out the Church. In fact it just grew and grew under his cruel persecution. You just can't wipe out the true Church of Jesus Christ.

I want you also to see that all these satanic attacks are taking place in the realm of the soul and of the body—in the realm of your feelings and emotions. They are designed to instill embarrassment, confusion, and fear. But there is a fairly easy answer to all of them: simply take it to the Lord in prayer. God will protect both body and soul from the devilish attacks of the enemy.

When the enemy of the Jews finally said, "We will kill them," Nehemiah again had an answer. In that beautiful verse 14, he says to his people, "Do not be afraid of them."

I want to tell you, friend, that today there is no reason to fear. God is working out his purposes through his people. God is still using his Church, and his Church is made up of individuals. I can tell you, as from God, "Do not be afraid!" God is working out his purposes.

Nehemiah adds, "Remember the Lord, who is great and terrible." How much do we think of our Lord? How often is our first reaction, "O Lord!" Or do we use God only as an emergency exit?

Like the sailor who had climbed to the top of the mast. Suddenly he fell. He cried, "God, help me!" Then he managed to get hold of a rope, and said, "God, you don't have to help me any more. I'm OK."

Nehemiah's injunction is for us, too. We must *always* think of the One who is with us, because he who is with us is far greater than he who is with the enemy. If you really know that, not just as an item of confessional faith, but as a daily working experience in your life, then God will always take fear away. He takes away the nervousness you feel as you face the enemy, because nervousness is also in the realm of the soul. That's what God wants to deal with first.

Nehemiah said to his people, "[Think of him who is with us, the great God of Israel], and fight for your brethren, your sons, your daughters, your wives, and your homes."

We all need to be reminded that the more we go on with the Lord, the more the enemy will be after us. In other words, the higher your experience with God, the higher the level of opposition. That is sometimes called the law of opposites. Paul put it in classic terms in Romans chapter 7, verses 21-25. Paul there declares, in effect, that the more he wants to do the will of the Lord, the more the devil fights against him. It's the law of opposites.

The intensity of satanic attacks increases in the same measure as you grow in Christ. You will always be attacked. You will be hit. You will be hurt and you will have wounds because you are not going to win over every temptation. You are not going to be the victor in every satanic attack.

Do you remember that Jesus, after his resurrection, showed himself to his disciples? What did he show to them? He showed them his scars. He said, "Look at my hands; look at my feet. Thomas, you don't want to believe it, so you look at my side; you can even put your hand in the scar there."

A famous missionary to India, Amy Carmichael, wrote many books and many poems about the Christian life. In one of her poems, she asked this question: "Can we have followed far, who have no wound or scar?"

Our one problem is, I think, that we are afraid of the battle. Sometimes the opposition is going to be so heavy that we will fall down. There is a greater defeat than falling down, and that is *staying* down. We have to get up and start fighting again!

Some years ago I was down and virtually out. We had a terrible crisis in our work, and I felt unable to cope any more. The pressure was such that I ran away from the trouble. I was really torn apart by the situation. One day, when I was alone, I again sought the Lord for a solution, and I suddenly felt God saying to me, "Andrew, you can give up your rights but not your responsibilities."

At that very moment I knew what I had to do. "Lord," I prayed, "I'll come back. I'll accept that." I got up off the floor and began serving him again.

I think we all have a responsibility to help our suffering brethren to get up off the floor. I see the collapse of people in prison like Wang Ming-Dao and now recently "Father Dudko" as the result of our failure. They should not have suffered that much. It is unfair toward them and it's the guilt of the rest of the Body that we did not carry their burden for them.

Wang Ming-Dao spent a total of twenty-three years in prison in China for his faith. When first imprisoned he was subjected to constant torture and brainwashing, until after fourteen months, he finally signed a confession that his opposition to the Three-Self Movement—the state-backed church—had been "counterrevolutionary." After his release, he was deeply disturbed emotionally about his actions, and finally he concluded that they had been caused by the brainwashing itself.

He rejected his "confession," and was immediately returned to prison. This time he was to remain twenty-one years and eight months. In January 1980 he was released again to join his wife, who also was imprisoned and had been released two years earlier.

Wang Ming-Dao said then: "I was a Peter many times, but never a Judas."

The devil does not want to stop you from going to heaven. The devil really doesn't care whether you go to heaven or hell; because your fate will not change his position in the universe. But the devil does want to stop you from the work of God, because in the measure in which God can use you for the building of his kingdom, the devil loses thousands in the universe. This is the big struggle in the world today.

We must remember that all the attacks we have studied in the life of Nehemiah and all the devilish attacks you have experienced in your own life also came to Jesus. The Bible says that no temptation has overtaken you that Jesus has not also met. The devil himself directed the attack on Jesus. It's interesting to note that those attacks, as recorded in Matthew, chapter 4, follow the same pattern as for Nehemiah. They take place in the realm of body, soul, and spirit.

After so many days of fasting in the wilderness, Jesus was hungry. And the devil said, "Tell those stones that they become bread so you can eat and feel better." How did Jesus react? He did not argue with the devil. Here is one mistake we often make. We think that we can win an argument with the devil. We never can, for the devil has 6,000 years of experience arguing with billions of people. He is smarter than we are. The only defense against the attack of the devil is the Word of God. That's what Jesus used. He said, "It is written, 'Man shall not live by bread alone.'"

Then comes the second attack. The devil took Jesus to the Holy City, right to the pinnacle of the temple which, at that time, overlooked the very deep Valley of Kedron. I understand that it was then 200 meters straight down, although today, while the same wall is still there, it is not nearly as deep anymore. The devil took Jesus up to the peak and let him look down. It would make anybody feel dizzy. The devil said, "Now, Jesus, if you use the Word of God, I can do the same.

Jump down, because it is written, 'He will give his angels charge of you,' and 'On their hands they will bear you up, lest you strike your foot against a stone.'" That is my paraphrase of Matthew, chapter 4, verse 6.

The devil is suggesting that he, too, knows the Bible. The devil can come in the disguise of an angel of light. If Jesus can quote Scripture, the devil can do that, too. We need to understand this tactic of the devil, because many attacks on us come wrapped up in a justification that seems to be based on the Bible.

Did you ever ask yourself that question: "Is what the devil quotes really from Scripture?"

If you have a reference Bible, it will refer you to Psalm 91, verses 11 and 12, as if the devil had quoted that passage: "For he will give his angels charge of you to guard you in all your ways. On their hands they will bear you up, lest you dash your foot against a stone." Now, does it say there what the devil said in Matthew, chapter 4?

No, it does not.

If the devil ever uses Scripture, he will twist and turn it. God's Word does not say what the devil quoted to Jesus in Matthew 4, because the devil omitted something.

It is the part of Scripture you leave out that will be your undoing. The truth that you *don't* take from Scripture will be your downfall.

The devil chose to leave out of his quotation the key words, "to guard you in all your ways."

If Jesus had jumped off that high wall, there would have been no angel to catch him. He would have landed on the rocks as a bloody mass because he had gone out of God's ways.

Do you see what the devil is after? In this case, he was trying to get the Jews off course, to scramble their compass so that it would lead them in the wrong direction, to get Nehemiah and his workers off that road on which they were going for God.

That could be the attack of the devil on our lives, too. And it is an effective attack. How many Christians know that they are doing the will of God? To be spiritual leaders, we must know that we are doing the will of God, or else we cannot build the wall.

Jesus replied, "Devil, it is written, you shall not tempt the Lord your God."

Does this mean we tempt God when we take a part of his Word but deliberately fail to apply another part?

The devil went on to a third temptation. He took Jesus to a high mountain and he showed him all the kingdoms of the world. And he said, "I will give all that to you." The devil knew that one day Jesus would rule all the kingdoms anyway, but he offered him a shortcut to the kingdoms of the world. He said, in effect, "Jesus, do not go to the cross; just bow down before me and I will give you all this glory."

Notice that Jesus did not dispute the claims of Satan over the kingdoms of the world. Satan is the prince of this world. Satan could have given all these things to Jesus. Let us, in turn, not be overanxious in our desire for the comforts and acclaim of this world. You can even spend too much time and energy working for your own country. So many nationalistic movements today rob the church of strength and faith. The real battle takes place on another level.

These attacks, three in a row from the devil, were not the only "temptations" of Jesus. Other attacks came from the Pharisees. An attack even came from his own disciple, Peter. Jesus saw them all as coming from one source. To the devil he said, "Be gone, Satan!" To Peter, he said, "Get thee behind me, Satan."

You would never say that to your friend, would you? But Jesus did! Because at stake was the kingdom of heaven. When you find yourself under attack, remember it is not just that one brick that you are privileged to lay in the wall; the whole structure of the kingdom of God is under attack.

That's why Jesus had no patience with anyone who tried to divert his attention. If God has done something for the world in Jesus Christ on which the salvation of the whole world depends, then I must be just as intolerant of every diversion— anything that dims my vision. We alone know the basic sickness of the world, and we alone know the cure. How dare I allow myself to be distracted from that great task?

The Apostle Paul stressed the "obedience of the faith." That's why Paul preached so much about the warfare. That's why Paul's body was covered with scars. He believed in the battle; he wanted to be in the battle; and he was ready to pay the price of the battle.

Paul was the constant target of the devil's attacks because, as in the life of Jesus, the devil wanted to stop the work of redemption. All of us who want to follow Jesus will have to go into that same battle. And Satan will attack you. In your body, in your soul, in your spirit. By far the fiercest attacks will be in your spirit. And I will tell you why this is.

The devil wants to kill the life of Jesus in you. All the attacks that come to me are not concerned about Brother Andrew as a person. I have no value in this world or in the kingdom of God. They are all directed against the life of the Son of God in me.

That is why every one of you is so extremely important. It is the *life of the Son of God in you*. That is the target of the devil's attack. Therefore all the commandments in the New Testament are not given to me, they are given to the life of the Son of God in me. That is also why I can do anything that the New Testament commands me.

We can indeed build the kingdom of God on earth! We can have righteousness in our own life. We can be used by God to build the wall.

TEN
COME TOGETHER—
WORK TOGETHER

The first three days after Nehemiah had arrived in Jerusalem, he tried to be as inconspicuous as possible. Then he began to do some very personal, independent research. In chapter 2, verses 11-16, we have already seen him going out on his donkey into Jerusalem at night to inspect the ruins personally. If we do not have the moral courage to inspect how bad things are, how can God ever use us to build things up? If you want a personal call, you have to do personal research.

Finally, in chapter 2, verse 17, he shares his burden with his friends. He says to them, "You see the trouble we are in, how Jerusalem lies in ruins with its gates burned. . . ." There is great power in sharing a burden with other people. You need to do so in order for other people to pray for you. You need to do so in order to get guidance from the Lord as to what you have to do, since he speaks through the constructive advice of fellow Christians. You need also to inform them because you need them as co-workers.

That's the necessity for Nehemiah's next sentence: "Come, let us build the wall of Jerusalem, that we may no longer suffer disgrace." He is saying, "Come, build with me. I cannot do it alone. I need everyone of you to take part." Individualism in Christian work is one of the greatest curses of the church today. It prevents us all from getting involved in the real struggle. We are a fellowship; we are a body. We cannot act independently of each other. We have to involve every member of the Church of Jesus Christ in the supreme task of world evangelism.

Politically speaking, the major problem in the world today is communism. What is the tremendous strength of communism today? It's this: that there are no spectators in communism. Everyone is involved in communism. Every Communist is a revolutionary. They don't talk about giving one-tenth of their income to the party—they have to give up to 90 percent of their income. If they don't do that, then their fellow colleagues or even their own relatives will betray them to the party.

Christianity has never achieved that kind of participation. In our Christian church life, 99 percent of the people are spectators. The only contribution they make is a small one in the collection plate on Sunday. If God is going to win in the world, then that situation has to change drastically.

As Nehemiah shared his burden, something happened. In verse 18, the people respond with their reaction. After Nehemiah has told them the good things God has done for him and their faith is thus strengthened, they say, "Let us rise up and build." Now, that's great! It's no longer Nehemiah saying, "Come, rise and build!" He is just standing back a little; he has shared the burden; he has told them about God's goodness. Now they catch the vision! That's revolution! That is a very important step in preparation—to learn that we need each other. We must do it together. We must show our solidarity with one another.

You and I should pray that that spirit of "Let us arise and build" will go into all Christianity, all over the world today. Much will have to happen before that will come true. If you look into any Christian hymnbook, you will find that probably 90 percent of all the well-known Christian hymns speak about "me" and "I," "my happiness," "my salvation," "my joy," "my place in heaven," "when I see Jesus," "when I go to glory." Did you ever notice that? What is the present-day trend in our new choruses and songs? As long as we talk and think and sing about "I" and "me," we will never be able to identify with the need nor be able to function as a Body.

Today we face a big struggle within the developing nations. We see oppressed nations wanting independence. There is nothing wrong with that; it is their right. The characteristic of the movement is the tremendous solidarity among the oppressed nations of the world today. They talk about "we"; they are united in their desire to be independent. Amazing strength! Oh, that the church would realize that same strength of identification and solidarity!

As soon as the people started working together in Jerusalem, opposition arose. Some people with different interests despised Nehemiah. They said, "What is this that you are doing? You are rebelling against the king." Nehemiah's response was a collective one: God is with us.

I just love his response in chapter 2, verse 20: "The God of heaven will make us prosper, and we his servants will arise and build; but you have no portion or right or memorial in Jerusalem."

So Nehemiah knows where to draw the line. There are people who will work with you, and you should work with them. But there are those people who will never work with you in bringing in a harvest of souls. Don't waste your time on them. God is calling enough people who will want to work with you to bring in the harvest of souls. Concentrate on the people who want to work with you.

There is a modern-day movement that talks about unity today. Some call it the ecumenical movement. Ecumenism always starts when things begin to go wrong. When the churches are empty; when they have lost their membership; when there is a lot of apathy among the people; when liberalism and modernism have taken over in theology; then all of a sudden they say, "Oh, let's all come together."

Well I know a beautiful story in the New Testament—in Luke, chapter 5. There Jesus said they must do some fishing, and they caught so much fish they thought the nets were going to tear apart. From the ship they called to other people, saying, "Come and help us!" Now, that's a different story, a completely different kind of ecumenism. When there is a harvest to be reaped, then please do ask others to help you.

The end of that story is recorded in verse 11. It says that, after they brought the ships to shore, they left everything and followed Jesus. That is the result: working together, building together, having a positive outlook on the future, obeying God, accepting leadership, and being willing to pay the price. For there is a price to be paid.

When you are building together, you share your faith; you share your resources; yes, you share your money, and you share your personnel. That's the way we must build—paying the price of working together—because that's the only way to get the job done.

I see in the way Nehemiah exerted his authority and leadership that basically he was a lonely person. He wasn't looking for fellowship; he was looking for fellow-workers. There was a task to be done, and when he said, "Come and let us arise and build," his personal enthusiasm carried through into the lives of the people who heard him.

As I said before, nothing great will ever be accomplished without enthusiasm. It means "be aglow with the Spirit," "be fiery in the Spirit." Therefore in the same way, we can say that without the Spirit of God burning in us, nothing great will ever happen. But once that Spirit has caught up with our own spirit, and we are united in our great aim and goal, then great things are bound to happen.

Where did Nehemiah start to build? In chapter 3, verse 1, it says, "Then Eliashib the high priest rose up with his brethren the priests and they built the Sheep Gate." You see, now everyone is going to work with his hands. That's why I say there is no difference between secular work and spiritual work. Here are the high priest and the other priests laying bricks and doing carpenter's work just like all the others are doing. All the work we do in the name of Jesus Christ is sanctified before God. Preaching is not any more important than typing letters in the office or keeping the accounts. We all need an equal share of the anointing of the Holy Spirit. Without that, nothing will be built for the kingdom of God.

Now comes one of the most fascinating sequences in Scripture. There are three key words that I have underlined in the Bible. Verse two of chapter 3 begins with the words, "And next to him the men of Jericho built. And next to them Zaccur the son of Imri built." And then a long sequence of the phrase "next to him." As I began to read this chapter with these three words marked, it turned into a song: "And next to him, and next to him, and next to him." How beautiful!

Just a few footnotes as we go along. In verse 8, it mentions one Hananiah, who was of the medical profession. But he was building the wall. God used men of all professions to build the wall. One next to the other; the doctor next to the psychiatrist, who is next to the pastor.

There is only one very sad note in this chapter. That occurs in verse 5, which begins by saying, "And next to them the Tekoites repaired; but their nobles did not put their necks to the work of their Lord." Oh, that is terrible! But of course the New Testament also notes, "For there are not many wise, not many noble." He didn't say there weren't any of them, he only said not many of them. Let's face it, dear friend. God builds his kingdom through ordinary men and women like you and me. That should make us feel good. God hasn't written us off.

In chapter 3, after verse 16 the word "next" does not occur again. From verse 16 on, the words "after him" occur many times and that turns into another song. From "next to him, next to him" to "after him, after him." Oh, let us build together! It makes a beautiful picture. All needed one another, and they knew it.

If I were inspector of the rebuilding committee, and were to check up on their rebuilding progress, do you think I would find a big gap of 100 meters where no one was working? No, I would not. This is how we ought to work in the world. We've got to do it together.

Right at the end of the chapter, there is one more word. I already said much about the word "next" and the word "after." In verse 32, we find the word "between." This is just in case there should be a somewhat bigger gap between workers, then somebody would step in between. Maybe that is your call today.

It is interesting to rewrite some chapters from the Bible in a manner similar to Nehemiah, chapter 3. Let me give you an example. Consider Romans 16:1: "I commend to you our sister Phoebe, . . . for she has been a helper of many and of myself as well." That's a tremendous testimony the Apostle Paul gives Phoebe. In this one chapter there are exactly ten different people described. If you write them all down in order like

Nehemiah did, you would say, "My, didn't the Apostle Paul have many co-workers." Yes, just like Nehemiah had; how else could he have built the wall?

In 1 Corinthians 16, verse 15, we read: "Now, brethren, you know that the household of Stephanas were the first converts in Achaia, and they have devoted themselves to the service of the saints." What a beautiful ministry. The Old English translation said they were "addicted to the saints." We think of addiction as something negative, but not when you are addicted to saints! Oh, the all-consuming love you can have for saints! That makes you open not only your heart but your home and your purse. There are more people mentioned in that same chapter.

You find another list in Philippians 4. In verse 2, Paul speaks about two women who need to be reconciled. These two women are having a quarrel. That's a terrible thing, but I'm so glad the Bible is honest. The Bible does not say that Christians never have a quarrel, because they may have a big difference of opinion. It may even get to boiling point. It's all been recorded in the Bible. Listen to what Paul says about these two quarreling women. "They have labored side by side with me in the gospel together with Clement and the rest of my fellow workers, whose names are in the book of life."

They have labored side by side! In other words, next to Paul is Euodia, side by side; and next to her, Syntyche; and next to her Clement, and next to him . . . . Let us build together. Paul had so many fellow workers that he could not take the time to list them all, but he says their names are in the book of life. Is your name in the book of life? Yes, as a believer of Jesus, but how about as a fellow worker?

Let's take one illustration—this one from the Book of Colossians, chapter 4, where Paul lists some of his fellow workers. In verse 11, he concludes one list by saying, "These are the only men of the circumcision among my fellow workers for the kingdom of God and they have been a comfort to me." So many activities in the Church of Jesus Christ in Paul's time had to go underground because of political pressure. In a number of places in the epistles, the writer had to camouflage or disguise the names of places or the names and functions of fellow workers. In this sense, he may feel it is too dangerous to speak openly about his Jewish brethren, so he says, "those of the circumcision." We have to be so careful in our work nowadays because of the opposition we encounter, for instance, in Communist countries, that we dare not name our contacts or the towns that they come from. The same applies to countries where there is either revolution, persecution, or strong nationalistic activities.

But what does Paul say about them? He remembers their names and then his heart grows warm all over again. He says, "They have been such a comfort to me." Paul, do you mean to say you needed comfort?

Can I tell you a secret? I know a little of what loneliness is. I remember times when somebody put an arm around my shoulder, and all I could do was cry.

In the early years of my ministry to Eastern Europe I thought I had gotten used to loneliness. Weeks alone at the wheel of my little Volkswagen had steeled me, I thought, for being isolated from my fellow human beings.

But when I arrived in the United States in 1965 for my first visit, I was knocked sideways with what happened to me. For many years I had fought against going to America because I felt that was the route many from Europe had taken to pick up finances for their work. Also, I wasn't going to spend the money people had given me for Bibles to buy an air ticket to America.

I changed my mind, however, when I met an American after a meeting in Holland. He had heard me preach and invited me over for a speaking tour. I hadn't realized at the time, but he was a fanatical anti-Communist who expected me to "slam the Commies" at my meetings. I suppose I should have guessed when I first arrived at his Bible school in the mountains, where he had his students running around with guns. He had told them the Communist invasion forces were at the Mexican border and could come at any time.

"If we don't fight, there is no hope for America," he declared.

We got off to a disastrous start. At my first meeting, I spoke about my experiences taking Bibles into Eastern Europe. He was so angry that I hadn't done any "Commie-bashing" that he canceled the rest of the trip and dumped me. I was so broke that I had to stay in the cheapest, most run-down motel I could find. Each morning I would go to a nearby shop and buy a quart of milk and possibly a yogurt. I would eat the yogurt with a shoe horn I had with me.

I lived like this for several days until Corry was able to wire me some money.

Eventually I got some bookings. I remember going to Denver to one of the biggest churches there. We had an emotionally moving service, with many people in tears as I described the plight of the suffering believers behind the Iron Curtain and showed slides to illustrate what I was saying.

At the end of the meeting, the pastor came to the pulpit and made an impassioned plea for the entire congregation to dig deep into their purses to pay for "new cushion covers for the pews." I couldn't believe it.

Then I was invited to speak at a large theological seminary. I used up my last cents to pay the air fare to get there. When I arrived I found that only three people had shown up—a professor and two students. No one even paid my expenses.

I had never felt so lonely in my life as I did then with all these selfish people. What was God trying to teach me? What good could possibly come out of this American nightmare? It just didn't seem to make any sense at all. But then the tide turned dramatically.

I met up with a couple of fine brothers, based in California. Through them I was invited to speak at some home churches throughout the state. Then one night, in Los Angeles, I went along to a meeting to hear a man called John Sherrill speak about his miraculous healing from cancer. Afterwards I was introduced to him and I discovered later that he had worked for *Reader's Digest* and was now with *Guideposts* magazine in New York.

"What are you doing?" he asked. I told him a little of the work and he seemed really interested and asked several penetrating questions.

"Look Andrew, would you have breakfast with me tomorrow at my hotel?" he asked.

I nodded, not telling him I had never been to a Hilton before in my life. Our breakfast meeting was really elevating for me. Our discussion lasted for three hours and he drank in my every word. This was the first genuine interest I had found in the suffering Church from anyone with whom I had spoken individually. Soon John was writing up the interview for *Guideposts* and suddenly the whole ministry began rolling. The interest it generated was phenomenal.

Eventually John, along with his wife Elizabeth, worked on the book *God's Smuggler*, which is now translated into thirty languages and is even secretly being sold in the Soviet Union and China. One of our contacts in China, who was at university in Peking, actually kept copies of the book under her bed along with the Bibles she was distributing to believers in the capital.

So the Lord used that time of terrible loneliness for good—and to eventually greatly further his work to the persecuted Church.

The ministry of comfort! Maybe that's all they ever did for Paul—just put their arms around him. But years later, Paul is in prison and he remembers them. Do you perhaps see a ministry for yourself?

Let me just make one more comment along this line. In verse 14 of that same chapter (Colossians 4), Paul refers to Luke as "the beloved physician." Paul had effected healings by the grace and power of God. If everyone was healed by faith and prayer, Luke would no longer be practicing. Undoubtedly, at the time this passage was written, Brother Luke is still working as a physician, and that's how all of Paul's fellow workers knew him—a faithful co-worker and physician.

Let's return to Nehemiah and the wall, because there is one more important question to be asked. When we are all building on that big wall, when the wall is high up and everyone has built his own part, how do you get those parts stuck together? That's a very interesting question, because there are many missions in the world that are working only in their own mission. But they are building for God.

I want to make it very clear that I am not criticizing any mission, but unfortunately missions often have no contact with other missions. They are building a part of the wall, but it has no connection to the other parts of the wall. How do we glue those two parts of the wall together? Well, we are going to need an extra lump of mortar, which I would call love. But there is a better way. Missions can build together.

The Open Doors mission works with many different organizations. We are each building one part of the wall; each of our works is absolutely different but does not need to be separate. The various bricks we are putting in our sections will overlap one another at the joint. For instance, when I need good people, or I see a new need, I go to some of the missions I have in mind—Operation Mobilization, Youth With A Mission, the Hospital Christian Fellowship, Wycliffe Bible Translators, and so on. We enjoy this type of fellowship, because we are building together. When the wall is finished, there will be no opening between the sections. That's why I believe missions should have fellowship together on the same level. There you share your vision.

In Nehemiah, chapter 4, verse 6, we read, "So we built the wall; and all the wall was joined together to half its height. For the people had a mind to work." Now they had been working for only a few weeks, and already half of the entire job was finished. If we want to work together, there is so much we can accomplish in a short time, but we must expect opposition. And there are particular dangers at the halfway point.

ELEVEN
DON'T DIALOGUE—
PROCLAIM!

At this point, special attacks come upon the person of Nehemiah.

If you will look at Nehemiah 6:15, you will see that the wall was completed in fifty-two days. Now that's marvelous! Only fifty-two days to finish a whole city wall! No wonder Nehemiah's enemies were in panic.

But the devil typically launches special attacks against those who are halfway through something. The halfway point in any project is a hard and dangerous point. We have started to build, but the end still seems a long way off. We have started to build, but there are problems and discouragements.

At one time I was a long-distance runner. I always found the halfway mark was the most difficult. You get so tired you want to give up. There is a barrier, a pain barrier, and you have to crash through. Then the second part is easy.

Many students studying foreign languages confess that after six to nine months they want to quit. They get terribly depressed. They are at the danger point.

Brother David, my friend and colleague who heads up our Open Doors work into China, met with Wang Ming-Dao in Shanghai shortly after his release in January 1980.

Pastor Wang, now age eighty, told David: "There is an ancient Chinese saying: 'There are many beginnings but few endings.' Everybody doing anything makes a start, but those who carry through to the end and completion are very few."

He went on: "Ahead God is leading and behind me God is defending. I am in the middle. What have I to fear?"

What indeed! Keep going, pressing on to the high calling of your Lord.

Now, with the whole world not yet evangelized; *now*, when God has given us so much promising potential; *now*, while we are right in the midst of the battle—that's when the devil attacks. What is going to decide the outcome? Will we take it to the Lord in prayer? Unless we pay the price of pressing on through to God, we will not make it.

Now that the enemy realizes Nehemiah just might accomplish what has been begun, his attack upon the life of Nehemiah is on a much different level. Sanballat and his friends realize that they have failed so far to dissuade the people, so in chapter 6, verse 2, they send a message to Nehemiah. "Sanballat and Geshem sent to me, saying, 'Come and let us meet together in one of the villages in the plain of Ono.' "

What are they suggesting? "Come let us talk together; let's have a dialogue."

When Nehemiah said, "I cannot come down," it is as if he meant, "I don't want to get down to your level." Nehemiah didn't even believe in dialogue. Nor did Jesus.

Dialogue is a very popular word today. We want to have a dialogue between East and West. We want to have a dialogue between Islam and Christianity. We want to have a dialogue between Catholics and Protestants. We want to have a dialogue between whites and blacks.

Dialogue is such an "in" word that we need to understand its implications. If I accepted dialogue with any person I could only do so on the assumption that he might be right and I might be wrong. I could only do so if I was convinced of his sincerity, if I deeply respected him.

Jesus has sent us to do the work of proclaiming the gospel, not to have a dialogue. Jesus came to die on the cross to defeat Satan once and for all. Jesus did not come to have a dialogue with the devil.

Jesus only acted upon principles. Then he sent his apostles

out to proclaim the kingdom of God. He didn't send them out to have a dialogue with heathenism.

The teachings of Jesus are clear: if any one of you will believe the message, whether in East or West, whether white or black, whether Catholic or Protestant; if you will believe in the Lord Jesus Christ, God will use you to build his kingdom. Do you see how this solves for you the problems you face today in the world? You work in another kingdom. You move on another level.

Now I am not criticizing people who work on the worldly level. I am not criticizing politicians and people who fight for the rights of oppressed nations. As a matter of fact, personally, I would tend to identify with them. When I spoke to Mr. Ian Smith, the then Prime Minister of Rhodesia, I said, "You must give me permission to go into the forbidden areas, because I want to go to those freedom fighters in Africa. I want to identify with them as people. I want to throw my arms around them and say, 'You are my brothers!'" That is what Jesus would have done. Unfortunately, nothing ever came of the request.

During the elections, however, several young Christians in Rhodesia used the opportunity to go into the bases where the guerrillas were staying to witness to them for Jesus. I agree with that wholeheartedly.

There is a principle to be observed. If I could visit guerrilla bases in Africa or Palestinian guerrilla camps in the Arab world, I would want to sit with them and identify with them as people, but I would not have a dialogue with them. If they wanted to take me down to a political level for dialogue, I could only accept that invitation if I had an alternative to their viewpoint. I could "dialogue" on a political level only if I could offer an alternative on that same level, but I am not working on that level.

I am not saying they are wrong; I am only saying that I work on another level, and I cannot come down because I am too busy. God has given me a program that is his kingdom. That does not mean it makes me better than they. It only means that I work on another level, with other kinds of people, with totally different methods, and with a totally different goal in mind. I am working for things that are eternal.

God has given me his work to do; therefore, I am not going to have a dialogue on a political level because, in so doing, I admit that my Christian beliefs are worth no more than their political philosophy. That would be a terrible lie! Our work is totally different. We work for the things of God.

That is also why you cannot have a dialogue between religions and Christianity—a dialogue, for instance, between Muhammedanism and Christianity. Because Christianity is not a religion. Did you know that? Christianity is a way of life. It is *walking with Jesus*. I can do that in any country; I can do it under any political regime. I can walk with God as Enoch walked with God thousands of years ago. And I can walk with God as all the men and women of the Bible walked with God.

Let me give you a practical illustration. Suppose I go to a Communist border and in my car I have Bibles. I have them because in the other country most Christians, even many pastors, have no Bibles. The border guard stops me; that is his duty. I expect him to serve his master well. His master tells him to destroy my Bibles. Well, that is his right. I don't love him any less for that. I can love anyone who is persecuting me, because he is only serving his master—he is in bondage to his master or he would not be doing what he is doing.

Now if I will only serve my Master well, I'll have no problem. So the customs officer says to me, "Sir, do you have any religious literature in your car?" Now, remember, I will never tell a lie. What am I going to say? I have Bibles and he asked about religious literature. Shall I say yes or shall I say no?

Shall I come down to dialogue?

If I say yes to him, then I am admitting that Christianity is a religion on the same level as all other religions. But Christianity is not a religion; it is a *way of life*. God has given us his Book to show us the way of life, and Jesus is the way and *the* life.

So I look this man in the eye, and, with a perfectly clear conscience, I say, "Sir, I have no religious books in my car." I refuse to come down to his level, to the meaning he is attaching to the phraseology of his political philosophy.

But of course that is my interpretation. He has another interpretation and he has a right to have his own interpretation. If he then finds that I have Bibles in my car, any number of things might happen. Depending on the country, I may even go to prison. But before I set out on that trip, I had to decide that I would be willing to go to prison for the sake of the message of the kingdom of God.

Now some brother will say to me, "Jesus had a dialogue with the woman of Samaria." Is that so? He did not have a dialogue, because he proclaimed to her the message of God's kingdom. He told her the truth about herself; then she asked questions about worshiping God. Jesus was proclaiming to the woman in Samaria, on her level, where she lived, in order to reach her.

Jesus applied the principle of identification. That's why I said I would love to go to those guerrilla bases. I can identify with the people there but that does not mean that I have to have a dialogue with them, because I am not going to offer them an alternative for their guerrilla ideals. I would want to proclaim to them the gospel of Jesus Christ, so that they can come up to the spiritual level of the kingdom.

Identification is living *where* other people live; it is not living *as* other people live. Jesus came down to earth to live where we live, but he did not live as we live. He didn't come down to that level of losing his relationship with the Father. In that sense Jesus never had a dialogue. The devil proposed a dialogue, but Jesus said, "Oh, no!" Jesus and the devil never sat around the conference table. They did not settle their differences in a debate. Jesus came to die on the cross, and by dying on the cross he defeated Satan.

I think there is something very humorous in this request for Nehemiah to come down and talk with his enemies. The dialogue was to take place in the plain of Ono, but when they invited Nehemiah, he said, "Oh, no!" He is not going to talk to them under any circumstances. In verse 4 it says, "And they sent to me four times in this way and I answered them in the same manner." Four times they said, "Let's talk"; four times he said, "Oh, no!" I like that! Our no should be as loud as our yes. The world is looking for that. Our yes to Jesus Christ should make us unmovable. In the measure in which we sound our yes for Jesus, in that same measure we should sound our no to the devil.

In verse 3, we have Nehemiah's most complete reply to his enemies: "I am doing a great work and I cannot come down. Why should the work stop while I leave it and come down to you?"

Nehemiah could see through his enemies' stratagem. They wanted to take away the leader so that all the followers would stop working. They wanted to talk and talk and talk until no time was left for work.

I like his answer: "I am doing a great work"!

Nehemiah, aren't you being a bit proud? Be careful here. If the housewife knows she is a good cook, and says, "I can cook well," is she proud? No, she is not. Pride in craftsmanship is not wrong. You know if you are a good doctor or a good nurse—you *ought* to know. You ought to know that you are appreciated for good work. Everyone who is busy doing God's will is busy in a great work.

What is pride? Pride in ownership—that is real pride. That is also the curse of the Western world. We are proud about the things that we have gathered around us. We are proud of the things that we can possess. That trait is corrupting our Western society. As a Christian you ought to know you are doing a great work, and that will help you not to be diverted by silly things and petty desires.

After Nehemiah's enemies have tried unsuccessfully four times to get him to step down for a dialogue, they intensify their attack. In chapter 6, verse 5, Nehemiah notes that "in the same way Sanballat for the fifth time sent his servant to me with an open letter in his hand."

The letter is one of accusation. If Sanballat could have called a press conference, he would have told the reporters that there were a lot of bad things to be said about Nehemiah. But the aim would not be to change the things that were supposedly wrong, but to frighten Nehemiah and his followers. Nehemiah recognized that (verse 9) "they all wanted to frighten us, thinking, 'Their hands will drop from the work, and it will not be done.'"

We'd call the letter Sanballat wrote "character assassina tion." If you cannot kill a person physically, you can tell other people what a bad fellow he is. If you can make people doubt his motivation, then he is finished.

I have had that happen to me. A woman in my little hometown in Holland began to write letters to other people telling them what a bad person I was.

She wrote one of these nasty epistles to me personally. I remember I was staying at the W.E.C. headquarters in Upper Norwood, London, when the letter arrived. As I read the accusations she had scrawled out so vindictively, I broke down and cried. I was in my bedroom, so I sank to my knees and sobbed, "God, how can I solve this problem? It's all lies. All these bad things she is accusing me of are not true."

But then the Lord showed me what to do. So I penned a letter back to my accuser. "Sister," I told her, "it's far worse than you have said. If only you knew my heart; it's much worse than your accusations."

That stopped the matter. After that she never wrote another bad letter about me. She knew the letter did not frighten me. You see, Nehemiah's enemies just wanted to make the Jews afraid. They wanted to take away their spirit, their willingness to work.

What is Nehemiah's reaction? At the end of verse 9, he prays, "But now, O God, strengthen thou my hands." Only God can keep you in the midst of such testing and false accusations.

The enemy noticed the effect of his prayer, because God answered Nehemiah and their hands were strengthened. Now there will be another attack. The fiercest attack possible. The next attack is the most vicious attack that one can experience in his Christian life and ministry. The devil tries the religious approach. When the devil becomes pious, you had better beware!

The biggest problem we face in our ministry is that of wolves in sheep's clothing. Beware of Western church leaders who receive the red carpet treatment from totalitarian regimes and then come back and say all is well. They become the biggest enemy of the suffering Church. Beware also of the so-called leaders from persecuted Eastern countries who tour the

West saying that all is fine in their countries. "There is no persecution," they say glibly. Take it from me: there *is* persecution on a massive scale, and these men are being paid by their Communist governments to mislead the gullible West.

We find recorded in chapter 6, verse 10, that Nehemiah went to visit a man who apparently was a friend, and this man, evidently seconding what many Jewish prophets had already said, suggested to Nehemiah, "Let us meet together in the house of God, within the temple, and let us close the doors of the temple; for they are coming to kill you, at night they are coming to kill you."

Now this is really a very insidious attack. The enemy has not been able to make Nehemiah go to the conference table for a dialogue, nor has Satan been able to damage his reputation, so now they propose to shut him up in the house of the Lord. The result will be the same: the work will stop.

Nehemiah gave a beautiful reply: "Should such a man as I flee? And what man such as I could go into the temple and live? I will not go in." Ordinary people who were not priests were not allowed to go into the temple. In other words, they were tempting Nehemiah to commit a spiritual sin. The attack against Nehemiah is now entirely on the level of the spirit, and that's the most dangerous level. Nehemiah's reaction is, "Should such a man as I flee?" In other words, he declares, "I am set in my responsibility: I have paid part of the price and I am ready to pay whatever else is necessary. If the rest of the price means paying with my life, then I will pay with my life, but I am not going to run away from my responsibilities."

I also want you to realize that such attacks will almost always be directed against the leader, because if the leader falls, the whole team is leaderless and therefore ineffective. Of course, there will also be attacks on the team members, but most of the attacks will be directed against the team leader. If the devil cannot get at him personally, then the devil will attack through his loved ones: his wife or his children. The result will be the same: the work will stop.

In the early days of my ministry I was traveling once in Hungary. My interpreter was a widow whose late husband had been greatly used by God as an evangelist.

"He was away at a revival campaign one time when I

became seriously ill," the woman told me. "He was sent a telegram saying that I was dying and asking him to return home immediately.

"He asked the Lord what he should do and knew the answer had to be that he should stay. 'I know the Lord will not let my wife die when I am away serving him. This is just a trick of the devil.'"

She told me that he stayed on and she was miraculously healed. I learned a lesson there. If God shows you how, you can refuse bad news on a personal level.

How many missionaries return home for that reason? They have given in to pressure at home instead of conquering by faith and staying on the job. If they had stayed on, the Lord would have solved the problem because He wouldn't let the devil win in such a devious way.

I can see, though, how Satan can attack us through our loved ones. Often, after a long trip away, I feel estranged from Corry and the children. I was away on one occasion for three-and-a-half months, and when I returned home, my children began to cry because there was a "stranger" in the house. They didn't recognize me. I was so upset that I began to cry too.

I know the pressures at times have been so great that Corry has even looked through the "situations vacant" section of the local newspaper and come up with secular work suggestions for us both.

However, we know really that that is not possible. God has called us to do a certain ministry and we have to keep pressing on. It is not easy at times, though. It was especially tough, for instance, when I was in Russia for six weeks and all the time believers there would use me as a shoulder to cry on. Then I came home and a stream of pastors would come and see me with their moral and spiritual problems. My problem was that I had no dry shoulder left. No resources to cope myself.

I would be exhausted, Corry tired, and the children irritable. Then the devil would say, "Andrew, why don't you give it all up and live a proper home life like other people?" I have had to make this particular matter a constant subject for prayer, because this is where the devil can cause havoc in our ministry.

The true state of affairs dawns on Nehemiah in verse 12: "And I understood, and saw that God had not sent him, but he had pronounced the prophecy against me because Tobiah and Sanballat had hired him." Nehemiah was not speaking about his Arab enemies; he was talking about Jewish "friends" who had been paid by his enemies to prophesy.

I am not going to say much about prophecy, but be very careful when people begin to prophesy about your personal life, and especially when somebody claims to have a prophecy that concerns your relationship to another person. These are often from the enemy, but they come through a so-called brother or sister, one who seems to be related to you through God. Nehemiah notes, "And I understood, and saw that God had not sent him." He had the spirit of discernment. He knew when a prophet was speaking from God, or from himself, or from the enemy.

In verse 13, the motive behind this tactic is stated: "For this purpose he was hired, that I should be afraid and act in this way and sin, and so they could give me an evil name, in order to taunt me." What was his reaction? The prayer of verse 14: "Remember Tobiah and Sanballat, O my God, according to these things that they did, and also the prophetess Noadiah and the rest of the prophets who wanted to make me afraid."

Note this verse carefully. Nehemiah prays against the enemies of God who are outside of Israel, but in the same sentence he mentions enemies who are within the camp. If the enemy were only on the outside, that would not be so difficult, but when the enemy gets inside, when your own friends begin to fight against you, and when so-called "spiritual" people speak as from God against you, that represents a real crisis.

Now this is an incredible development within that small circle of Nehemiah's friends inside Jerusalem, before the face of God, that there should be those so much under the influence of the evil one that they would prophesy against Nehemiah and his great work for God. It should make us all very cautious, because if it could happen *then*, it can happen *today*. What a need there is for all of us to have that spirit of discernment and to be sure of the will of God for our lives!

Once the devil begins to attack you on the spiritual level, it means that you are doing a very important work for God, but it also means that you are in very serious danger. You had better know your God. You had better know the Scriptures, otherwise you will be without an answer.

Now this old world is full of confusion, and that makes it all the more important that I should be building for God in the end times. The easiest thing to do in this confused world is to flee. You can flee to the busy-ness of your own profession; you can build a little wall around your family and flee into it. You may want to flee from your responsibility. But before you do, remember Nehemiah's cry, "Should such a man as I flee?"

I am reminded of that great reformer, Martin Luther. When he was to appear before the emperor in the city of Worms, his friends all advised, "Don't go there, Martin. They will finish you off there. You must flee!" He replied, "You can expect from me anything save fear. I shall not flee! My conscience is a prisoner of God's Word." When he stood before the emperor he said, "Here I stand; I can do no other. God help me!"

Are you in the place where you can say, "Here I stand; I can do no other"? Then you are a prisoner of Jesus Christ. If you are a prisoner of Jesus Christ, you can be nobody else's prisoner.

Luther translated Isaiah 28, verse 16, into German this way, "He who has faith does not flee." I think that is a beautiful translation. If you put all your faith in God, you will not run away from your responsibilities.

The responsibility you have is to build a wall! The responsibility you have is to serve God. The responsibility you have is to fight for your brethren, to fight for your families, and to fight for your homes.

TWELVE
BE AS PRACTICAL
AS YOU ARE
SPIRITUAL

One of the most appealing things about Nehemiah is that he was a practical man. Oh, he was also a deeply spiritual man, a great man of prayer as we have seen. But his leadership qualities included some very practical, down-to-earth, business-like characteristics—traits we sometimes mistakenly fail to link with those persons who are truly spiritual giants.

We have already mentioned Nehemiah's careful planning, and we need to learn from him in this. You should plan and organize ahead of your actions.

Nehemiah was also a cautious man. Please don't think that boldness and caution conflict with each other.

Daniel also displayed this characteristic when he was in the lions' den. He was bold, but he was also cautious. He certainly didn't antagonize the lions by pulling their tails. I once related this story to a medical doctor in Yugoslavia. He laughed and added: "And he certainly didn't brush their teeth, either, Andrew. That would have been asking for trouble."

I believe it is unscriptural to tempt the enemy. It's bad enough when he tempts you, but if you bait him you've lost. For instance, when we take Bibles through hostile borders we don't put them out on open display for the guards to spot immediately. That would be asking for trouble.

I know of one mission taking Bibles to Eastern Europe who always leave their Scriptures in a place where they can be spotted easily. They don't believe in hiding them. Sadly, they hardly ever get any of them through, which to me makes the whole operation rather pointless.

Nehemiah was both bold and cautious. But bold Nehemiah did not step into the battle without thinking ahead.

Note chapter two, verse 11. It says, "So I came to Jerusalem and was there three days." And verse 12: "Then I arose in the night, I and a few men with me; and I told no one what my God had put into my heart to do for Jerusalem. There was no beast with me but the beast on which I rode." Nehemiah did not make his inspection on the first day or on the first night after his arrival. I think I know why he delayed. He didn't want to arouse unnecessary suspicion on the part of his enemies. Many people had seen him arrive in this very poor city. He undoubtedly appeared to be a very rich and influential man. So everybody was watching to see what he was going to do. For three days, he did nothing, and then the people stopped thinking and talking about him.

There was another reason, too, I think. As a man of God, with a single desire to do the will of God, he constantly sought confirmations from the Lord. I know from my own experience that I would do this when I would leave my home in Holland and go to Eastern Europe. I first of all made the decision to go because I believed God had put it in my heart to do so. But I would always ask for at least two confirmations. That is a scriptural thing to do, but I still do not understand whether it is an indication of faith or of unbelief.

Do you remember the story of Gideon? Gideon knew what he had to do for God, yet he said, "Lord, I want you to give me a sign." He put out a fleece at night. The first night he said, "If the fleece is wet and the grass is dry, then I will take that as a confirmation of God's call." And that's exactly the way God did it.

So Gideon should have been confident now, but he said, "Lord, I am very sorry about this, and I want you to forgive me in advance, but I am going to ask for one more sign. I will put out that fleece again, and if tonight it is just the other way around, I will have faith enough."

Many people say Gideon was not a man of strong faith, because he should have obeyed the first time God told him what he wanted him to do. But he asked for an extra sign; he wanted extra confirmation, and when the Lord gave it he said, "Lord, I want one more confirmation." Was that an indication of unbelief?

What do you think? I feel it takes a lot of faith to believe that God will give a confirmation. So I say that even asking for a confirmation is an expression of faith. Of course you can never have enough faith. I always ask for one or two confirmations on every trip, even if these confirmations have to come while I am traveling toward one of the difficult countries.

One day I left my home in my little Volkswagon to go to Hungary. I stopped in a place close to Frankfurt, where there is a very fine Christian fellowship. I knew there would be a prayer meeting that evening, so I was going to pray there with them. When I came into the meeting, the leader of that group said, "Andrew, one of our older sisters is very ill; would you please go and visit her?"

I said, "I would love to visit her."

I went to her home and, as I entered her room, she said, "Hello, Andrew, are you there?"

I said, "Yes, and I am glad to see you."

She said, "I was expecting you today." I was astonished!

She continued, "Last night God told me that you would come this way."

Now here I had one of the confirmations I wanted, but I still wanted one more confirmation. Now you may say, "Brother Andrew, you are not a believer." Yes, but that's the way I am, you see. I just need a few more confirmations. I need faith in order to do things that without faith I could not do.

On that trip, as I came to the Hungarian border, there was fear in my heart. Now, maybe you never have fears, but I often have fear in my heart. I am not a brave man and I was there all by myself. I had a lot of things with me that normally I would not be allowed to take into the country. Besides, it was not tourist season in Hungary, so I would probably be about the only foreigner in a foreign car traveling around that entire communistic country. I intended to preach in many churches throughout the country and I had always had very large meetings, even revivals, in Hungary.

Now I was at the border and I was afraid. I did not want to cross into Hungary, because I knew that if there was fear in my heart, then there was no faith, because fear and faith cannot live in one heart.

As I came very close to the border, perhaps only 100 yards away from it, I could see all the barbed wire, the watchtowers, and the people with machine guns. Frankly, I was afraid, so I turned my car around and I drove back to the nearest village. I checked into a little hotel and there I spent two days in prayer and fasting, because I wanted to have one more confirmation. I needed something to take away my fear.

I don't know if you understand my problem, but perhaps one day in your life you will come to appreciate it. I just had to know one more thing from God, and I was determined to stay there until God would speak to me. I spent much of my time, of course, reading the Bible, and soon God spoke to me through his Word. All my fears left my heart. I ordered a good meal, packed my suitcase, and drove off to the border.

I crossed the Iron Curtain. God gave me a wonderful time in Hungary, but first I just needed to wait on the Lord.

I have even canceled trips when the Lord didn't give his seal of confirmation on them. I always have to wait upon the Lord.

That is what Nehemiah was doing in chapter 2, verse 11. Of course, he knew why he was in Jerusalem. He could have started building the wall on the first day, the first hour after his arrival, but that would have become a big flop. Let's learn to wait on the Lord. Let's give God one or two or as many opportunities as you need to tell you exactly what his will is for you. Only then can we make clear decisions; only then can we be truly successful in the work of the Lord.

Nehemiah also has a healthy sense of realism. In chapter 4, verse 9, we find this: "And we prayed to our God, and set a guard as a protection against them day and night." You see, you can become so overspiritual that you say, "Well, God has to do everything," But that would be very unscriptural. You have got to bring your need to God, but then, in many cases, God will say, "OK, now you answer your own prayer."

Nehemiah had to respond to a great threat against the people who were rebuilding the wall. He prayed about the situation, but immediately after the prayer, he arranged a guard, a system of protection. Isn't that what we all do, really? When we go to sleep at night, we commit ourselves to the Lord, we ask his protection over us—but that doesn't mean that we do not lock the door!

You have to be realistic. You must be spiritual on one hand, realistic on the other; when the two meet, then you are a balanced Christian. Actually, I should not imply that the spiritual and the realistic are different or do not agree. They do agree, but you've got to bring them together.

You trust the Lord for your health, but when it's cold you put on your coat. You expect God to give you a strong body, but you make sure that you get enough food. That is really being spiritual. If you neglect the care of your body, or if you neglect the care of your family, that would be very unspiritual. I find in Nehemiah that healthy realism of a man of God.

The spiritual and practical aspects of the man of God are also illustrated by the fact that Nehemiah had the faith for such a big undertaking—a faith God gave him. Yet every time he faces a problem, his first reaction is prayer. Prayer is a realistic response, admitting that he cannot solve the problem alone. Only God can solve the problem. The moment he asks God to solve the problem, in that moment he sees the answer. That's exactly how God answers prayers.

In chapter 4, verse 10, the men of Judah complain that the strength of the burden bearers was failing, there was much rubbish, and they would never be able to finish the work on the wall.

It is a special gift that a man has, to see when people are overburdened, a gift that leaders must have. It's so easy to drive people on, on the basis of your own determination or fanaticism, without seeing that they are getting tired. But Nehemiah took note of the fact that the people were getting tired, and he came up with a solution.

The real nature of the complaint was that, since the people were becoming tired, the enemy would be able to come in and kill them. In verse 13, Nehemiah recounts, "So in the lowest parts of the space behind the wall, in open places, I stationed the people according to their families, with their swords, their spears, and their bows." He arranged them in such a way that they no longer would feel threatened because of their tiredness. In other words, he rearranges his team so that they get rid of their frustration.

It's a special ability for leaders to see problems develop in the team, to find out why those problems arise, and then to find a solution for the underlying problem. That is a God-given and Nehemiah had it.

In chapter 5, verses 1-5, Nehemiah faces another problem. It's about food and the very essential problem of keeping alive. Some of the people had been forced to take mortgages on their possessions or to pledge their children as security for the food they had to buy to keep alive. Others were borrowing money to pay taxes. The result was that some of the people were amassing great wealth and others were getting poorer all the time. It's a typical worldwide problem, and particularly difficult when it involves relationships within a very small community. The wonderful thing is that Nehemiah, even though he is burdened by the responsibility he feels for rebuilding the wall, can see and understand the problem, and also have the courage to deal with the problem. In verses 6 and 7, he recounts, "I was very angry when I heard their outcry and these words. I took counsel with myself. . . ." He dealt with the problem. That is exercising the authority of a leader—when you point to the guilty one and defend the victim; when you correct a wrong situation and tell both sides what to do.

The strong character of Nehemiah is displayed clearly as he deals impartially with the people involved. Verse 7 continues, "I took counsel with myself, and I brought charges against the nobles and the officials. I said to them, 'You are exacting interest, each from his brother.'"

Think of it! Nehemiah is tackling the nobles; he is pointing his finger at the leaders of the nation. It's easy to point your finger at people on the lowest social and political levels. Anyone can accuse followers. If something goes wrong you can always say the laborers made a mistake. It takes great moral courage to say that the leaders are wrong. That's what I call impartiality: it makes no difference who is the guilty party; you confront them anyway. Do we care enough to confront both friend and foe?

I admire Nehemiah greatly for stepping into this situation.

The nobles were developing a system of capitalism which forced the poor people to borrow money, and the rich people could demand interest on the money they had loaned. But the Jewish law forbade them to take interest on money borrowed from brothers. The Jews were allowed to take interest on money borrowed by foreigners, but they were not allowed to take interest from their brethren. So when the rich leaders of his time did this, Nehemiah said, "You are wrong."

Frankly, I wondered how there could have been any rich people at all. Isn't it amazing that in such a poor society, as in Jerusalem at that time, where almost everybody was poor, there were still some rich people. Why didn't those rich people do something about the situation in Jerusalem before Nehemiah arrived? You will seldom find rich people who have the love of God in their hearts. If they really had the compassion of Jesus in them, they would have shared their wealth with the poor people long ago, just as many men and women of God have done in the history of the church.

Nehemiah did not make himself popular, I suppose, by speaking out against the nobles. But he had not left the king's service and gone off to Jerusalem for the sake of popularity. None of the prophets was popular; Jesus was not popular— that's why they crucified him. Do you want to be popular? Then you should go into entertainment or politics.

Nehemiah was seeking the welfare of his people. His heart was beating for those people, so much so that he couldn't care less for his own comfort or reputation. Is that quality of character already working in you and in me?

THIRTEEN
GOD HAS SAID

Nehemiah, the visionary, the leader of his people, planned carefully everything about the construction of the wall of Jerusalem. I assume he made the assignments in the building program. Significantly, his account of the work in chapter 3 begins with the priests building the Sheep Gate. The entire wall is to be built, and there are many different gates. Why does Nehemiah start the building program at the Sheep Gate?

This gate has special importance, because it is the gate through which the sheep are taken in as they are on the way to the altar. The first thing to be restored was the sacrificial lamb at the altar.

That has to be first with us, too—the Lamb of God who takes away the sin of the world, the message of the blood of Jesus Christ. That alone cleanses us from all sin and unrighteousness. It is only in the heart, cleansed by his blood, that God can impart faith. Is there no faith in your heart, perhaps because you do not know the Lamb of God? That's why God cannot give you faith.

Is there still fear in your heart? Fear and faith do not live together in one heart. Faith is not the absence of doubt, but the conquest over doubt, fear, and insecurity.

That's why the Sheep Gate had to be the first thing repaired in Jerusalem. Faith had to be restored in all the people. There had to be a cleansing from their sin, daily.

In all our ministry, we must be sure that we build on the basis of Jesus Christ. Jesus Christ is our only foundation for ministry. There is no sense in building any wall if we don't have that foundation. Whatever we are going to do in this world of ours, if the basis is not Jesus Christ, the Son of God, then we are only dealing with the symptoms of world problems, not with the issues.

The Sheep Gate points toward Jesus, and whatever we begin, we must first point people toward Jesus. We cannot do that unless we know Jesus Christ ourselves. We must know that Jesus is the central person in our lives and that, whatever we say, the theme will always be Jesus. We may not even be able to mention his name, but we will still speak about Jesus.

Let me say a little more about Jesus because I feel that we have been speaking more about Nehemiah throughout this book than we have been about Jesus. In Ephesians, chapter 4, verses 11 and 12, we read, "and his gifts were that some should be apostles, some prophets, some evangelists, some pastors and teachers, to equip the saints for the work of ministry, for building up the body of Christ." In Christ there is also a building going up. In verse 13, the building goal is stated: "Until we all attain to the unity of the faith and of the knowledge of the Son of God, to mature manhood, to the measure of the stature of the fulness of Christ."

In this passage in Ephesians a number of the ministries within the church are mentioned: apostles, prophets, evangelists, pastors and teachers. Jesus was all of these. Jesus was an apostle (Hebrews 3:1). Jesus was a prophet (Acts 3:22). Jesus was an evangelist (Luke 4:18). Jesus was a teacher (John 3:2).

It is interesting that, while Jesus was a teacher, he never said, "I am the good teacher"; he was a prophet, but he never said, "I am a good prophet." What did he say? He said, "I am the Good Shepherd." That means, "I am the good pastor." The pastor—the shepherd—is the one who feeds the flock.

I believe that is also why they began building at the Sheep Gate. Before we can continue to build in the kingdom of God, we must be fed by the Good Shepherd. Jesus, the Good Shepherd, feeds the flock, and if we, as leaders, want other people to work with us in the kingdom of God, our first aim should be to feed the flock. Our first responsibility is not to tell them what to do; that's not what we're experts in, anyway. Feed the flock!

How do we feed the flock? In John 10:15 we read how Jesus did it. He said, "I lay down my life for the sheep." In 1 John 3:16, we find this tremendous secret: "By this we know love, that he laid down his life for us." But the verse doesn't stop there. It also says, "And we ought to lay down our lives for the brethren." That's why they first had to build the Sheep Gate.

Do you remember that interesting conversation between Peter and Jesus after his resurrection? It is recorded in the Gospel of John, chapter 21, "Peter, do you really love me?" That's a searching question. Three times Jesus repeated the question, "Do you really love me?" He seemed to be implying, "You may have to pay a price for it."

Peter answered, "Yes, Lord, I do. You know I do. Why do you ask me? Why do you ask me three times? Don't you believe me? Don't you take me seriously? I do love you!"

What did Jesus say? "Then, feed my sheep." But he gave him nothing to feed them with. Peter had to be broken bread in the hands of the Master. Peter had no other resources; no other resources than the Man of Sorrows who, as the Great Shepherd, laid down his life for the sheep. He said, "Now, Peter, you do the same."

When Jesus says to you, "Feed my sheep," he gives you nothing to feed them with. Do you know why? Because *they should feed on you!* Through your prayer and devotion and Bible study, you should have a surplus of the love of God, enough for other people. It is the giving of yourself to others that will feed them.

"Feed my sheep." Jesus is the Lamb of God, and yet he is the Good Shepherd. We are the sheep, and yet we are shepherds. We are the building, and we must first build the Sheep Gate.

This concept of giving yourself is revolutionary. Jesus started a revolution—the revolution of love. In every other revolutionary movement in the world today, revolutionaries kill those who oppose them. What the world needs is a revolution of love: you give your life so that the other will live. That is the revolution of Jesus. What kind of revolutionary do you want to be? It depends on how much you really love him.

Nehemiah started the rebuilding of the wall at the Sheep

Gate because he knew the people would need, first of all, cleansing from sin. He knew they would need the faith that could come from a cleansed heart in order to complete the building. He knew that his people, too, had to come to the point of realizing that, because of the grace and love of Almighty God, they had no rights—only responsibilities and marvelous privileges!

Has the Sheep Gate been built into your life? Then you can go on to rebuild the other gates. That's what Nehemiah and the people of Jerusalem did. They completed all of the wall in fifty-two days.

When Nehemiah looked at the finished wall and gates, he thought, "I have a problem now; there are no people living in there. Why should we have built a wall and not have people inside to enjoy the security of the wall?"

What does Nehemiah do? In chapter 7, verse 5, he finds the book which listed the genealogy of all the people. He is going to check to see which of the people should live in Jerusalem.

Now we begin by saying that Nehemiah had an inquisitive mind; he wanted to know. Because he was honest enough to ask questions, God gave him a vision. He is obviously the same Nehemiah as he was back in the palace at Susa. He says, "Give me the book; I want to see whose names are written in that book."

That leads me to a very important analogy. God's Word tells us that there is a Book of Life. In the Book of Life, God writes every name of those who make a decision for Jesus Christ. No one is entered into the Book of Life by being born as a baby into the world. Being born in a Christian family does not entitle one to have his name placed in the Book of Life. If I were born in a stable, that would not make me a horse. If I were born in a biscuit factory, I would not be a biscuit today. Being born in a Christian family does not make me a Christian.

It is a tremendous blessing, though, to be born in a Christian family. It gives you a wonderful start in life to have a praying father and mother. But in this life, the moment has to come when you make your own decision for Jesus. Everyone, even though brought up in a Christian family or in a church, has to make that personal decision.

A lot of people have been involved in church work; they've

done much good in this world. They have been building on the wall, side by side, with us. Now God asks, "How about the Book? Is your name in that Book? Are you entitled to live in Jerusalem?"

That is a question that I must ask you. Have you made a personal decision for Jesus Christ as Savior? Do you know that all your sins are forgiven and that Jesus lives in your heart? Do you know that your name is written in the Book of Life? Do you really know this on the basis of your own personal decision? You must enroll in the Book of Life. Have you done that?

If you say, "Brother Andrew, I've never really done that; I've never made a personal decision for Jesus Christ; I always thought I was a Christian, but since you have said these things, I see I'm not a Christian. I'm not sure my sins are forgiven. I don't have that confidence; I don't know that, if I died today, I would go to heaven." If that is a picture of your life, then I want you to make that simple decision for Jesus now.

Chapter 7 of Nehemiah concludes, "And when the seventh month had come, the children of Israel were in their towns." I want you to be inside, too.

FOURTEEN
RESTORING
THE AUTHORITY
OF THE WORD

We come now to the most important contribution Nehemiah made to his people. The building of the wall was a tremendous achievement. Governing his people over a period of years, as an examination of the chronology in Ezra and Nehemiah will reveal he did, was also a different task requiring all the talents of a great leader.

But there was another assignment for Nehemiah, even more crucial than either of these. Turn to chapter 8. The wall had been finished. The gates were all in place. The people had all been checked out against the book of genealogy, to see who should live and work there. What else was there to do?

The most important contribution Nehemiah made to his people was still to come, an act more important than building the wall, although the wall had to be built first.

In Nehemiah, chapter 8, verse 1, it says, "And all the people gathered as one man into the square before the Water Gate." They were there with a sense of expectation, because they realized something important had to come from God. How were they going to preserve their society? How would they prevent the enemy from destroying the walls again? Now that so many had returned from exile, how could they live together in harmony, keeping that tremendous blessing which God had given them?

Nehemiah's great contribution comes at the Water Gate.

He restores the authority of the Word of God.

There is no greater contribution that you or I can make for the world today, than to lead the world back to the authority of the Word of God.

You can only establish the authority of the Word effectively if you are a man of one Book—a man who believes the Book, who acts upon the truths of the Book, who studies the Book, and who will pass on the Book.

I have traveled all over the world. I have been in all the countries of revolution. I have also been in many Western countries where people are filled with fear. They have asked me, "Brother Andrew, which way are we going?" They believe that nothing can slow down the revolution.

I disagree. There is one thing that can stop it. I have discovered in my observations that no nation has gone under to revolution where the Word of God has central place. No individual Christian who has the Word of God in the center of his life, has been destroyed by the devil.

I want to speak for my God today. I want to commend his Book to you. If this Book goes through you—that's something more than you going through the Book—then you will be a strong Christian. If your faith is built on this firm foundation, who can shake you? If you know the truth of this Book, how can anyone ever turn you away from Jesus?

You don't have to go to Bible school to become a man of the Book. All you need is the Book of God. John Wesley cried out, "Give me the Book of God at any price!" He knew that this Book was the answer to the world's problems.

He *had* the Book. He also had fellow workers who traveled and preached with him. Those young evangelists were on fire for Jesus Christ. The average age at which evangelists died in the time of John Wesley was thirty-two years—burned out for Jesus! They had only one goal—preach the Word.

Because John Wesley had the Book of God and liberty to teach the message of the Book and had followers who preached the Word of God, God saved Britain from the French Revolution. The only way God can save our nation from atheistic revolution; the only way he can save us from anarchy, is by a return to the Word of God.

We do not have to come down to the level of those people

who fight political systems; we are not fighting against governments. If you should encounter a radical who demands your attention and insists on telling you all that he is against, ask him first what he is for. Ask what alternative he has to offer. If he has no alternative based upon God's righteousness, please don't waste your time in listening to his message.

You will recall that that's what the enemies of Nehemiah wanted. They wanted to waste his precious time. Their only aim was to get him to stop the work. The only task God has called you and me to do is to work in his kingdom. All the attacks of the devil on your life, including the attacks on your body and the invitation for a dialogue, are all intended to stop you from working for God's kingdom.

Let us examine carefully the story of the gathering at the Water Gate. In chapter 8, verse 3, it says that the Word of God was read "from early morning until midday, in the presence of the men and the women and those who could understand; and the ears of all the people were attentive to the book of the law." They had a tremendous reverence for the Word of God.

How much do we really honor the Word of God? How much does it hurt us when God's Word is being attacked?

In verse 5 it says, "Ezra opened the book in the sight of all the people, for he was above all the people; and when he opened it all the people stood." Whenever I have opened the Book in Russia, the people stand. They would never sit when I read the Word of God to them. It's what you should do when the King begins to speak to you. You stand to attention, and you listen.

What else did they do? Verse 6 describes their response: "All the people answered, 'Amen, Amen,' lifting up their hands; and they bowed their heads and worshiped the Lord with their faces to the ground." They lifted their hands to heaven. They bowed their heads. And they worshiped the Lord.

They rejoiced and they worshiped God. Now God is not worshiped only when we shout our amens. You accomplish as much worship in the quietness of your own heart. But they had found a way to express their love and their joy to God.

Perhaps I speak as a Dutchman now, with too much of a Calvinistic background, but if you always manage to hide your feelings toward God, then you'd better look around in heaven for a big refrigerator! We have too many deep-freeze Christians.

I have a pastor friend in Holland who spoke once on the glories of the new earth and the new heaven. He preached for more than an hour on that theme, and in the end almost wept. He said to his people, "I have told you the most beautiful things about the future and you sit there in your black Sunday clothing with your long faces. I have not seen one smile. You act as if you don't believe the promises of God."

Can we not react when God tells us something? If we cannot laugh when God gives us a wonderful blessing, then we cannot weep when God shares a need with us. The one who cannot laugh, cannot weep.

Nehemiah wept. That's how this whole business of rebuilding the wall started.

Now we see him with his hands in the air, praising God.

Jesus wept. Jesus laughed. Jesus had a perfect sense of humor. Let's be like him.

The people at the Water Gate were overwhelmed by the love of God and by the fact that at last they had the Word again in their midst. Then they began to weep. Of course, they were still praising God, but their emotions were deeply involved in the expression of their faith.

So they began to weep, but Nehemiah, in verse 9, said, "Do not weep, this is a holy day for the Lord your God."

If you have ever done what I have done—place a copy of this Book in the hands of a pastor in Russia who had never had a Bible of his own—you would have seen what I saw: tears of joy. When you are in a situation where you have lost everything and you hear the words of God, you weep.

Some years ago, I was involved in a terrible air crash in the mountains of Colorado. The accident took place in a small plane, close to Salida Airport. The pilot took off all right, but then as we were climbing in the thin air at that high altitude, the engine cut out and we began losing height at great speed.

"What's going on?" I urgently asked Don, the pilot, as we fell downwards.

"We're crashing. . . ."

All I can remember is a terrific pain in my back and Don,

who by now had a gaping head wound, saying, "Andrew, get out and run. The plane could explode at any moment."

I somehow edged my way out of the wrecked plane, and began to run and then collapsed just yards away. I had broken my back in two places. As I lay there in agony, I knew that explosion or not, I could not move an inch further. It was then I noticed that we had crashed within yards of a ravine.

"Thank you Lord for sparing our lives," I gasped as the pain enveloped my whole body.

Soon an ambulance arrived, and one of the rescue team turned out to be a Pentecostal minister. He soon had phone messages going across the country asking for prayer for us. Kathryn Kuhlman and Jamie Buckingham were in a conference when they were interrupted with the news. Soon they had all the delegates in believing prayer for us.

I managed to phone Corry in Holland, from my hospital bed, and she was soon at my side. I was lying there in the hospital in great pain and she would sit beside me for ten hours a day. All she did was read from the Book. It was all I wanted to hear. I wasn't interested in knowing whether it was raining or whether the sun was shining. The Word of God! I think half the time I just had tears rolling down my cheeks. Ah, the Book, the Book—give me the Book! I had constant revival in my soul as long as I was in pain.

When I could finally get up, my wife had to teach me to walk again. And soon I was back into the work. Once again I had many problems. The revival in my own soul had stopped. I was no longer spending those hours in the Word.

You remember the story of those American prisoners of war in North Vietnam—what did they do when they were being interrogated and tortured every day? I spoke to some of them. They told me, "Our major project was to reconstruct the Bible from memory." The Book must come back in us!

In verse 10 there is a very important statement. Nehemiah had reminded them that this was a day of great joy, because they had the Word of God back in their midst. He said, "Let the joy of the Lord be your strength." He also said, "Send portions to him for whom nothing is prepared." Now that is the task of our Open Doors mission—to send portions of the Word of God to those for whom nothing has been prepared.

When we take the Word of God to people, we want to take them not just the printed Book, but also the Word of God as it has become incarnate in us. You ask, are there still people who have no Bible available? Two thousand languages in the world do not have one verse. In Russia alone, 100 language groups have no word of Scripture in their language. There is a country in Europe that does not have the Scriptures. It is Albania. Almost 2,000 years ago the Apostle Paul was there, but to this day we still haven't prepared a whole Bible for Albania. No wonder they have closed all the churches and apparently killed off all the Christians so that there is no trace of religion in Albania. The country is the first officially proclaimed atheistic state in the world.

When we bring back the Word of God, then we will have revival. We will once again learn the fear of the Lord. Then the Word will end divisions; it will stop backbiting and gossiping. It will finish criticism because we will tremble at his Word which forbids such things. Oh, the Word of God, study it, dear friends!

In chapters 8, 9, and 13, there are nine instances in which Nehemiah made very important decisions on the basis of God's Word. Some of these decisions were related to problems between rich people and poor people, or problems about life and conduct. They were solved upon the basis of the authority of God's Word.

There is so much you can do with the Word of God.

Do you remember the first temptation to sin in Paradise? It had nothing to do with sex. And nothing to do with the apple. In all of Genesis an apple is never mentioned.

All the devil did there to Adam and Eve was to make them doubt the truth of God's Word: "Has God said?"

Today I say, "God *has* said." He has chosen you. He has ordained you that you should go forth, that you should bear fruit, and that your fruit should remain.

God has said: "Go into all the world and preach the gospel."

God has said: "Make disciples of all nations."

God has said: "Strengthen what remains and is at the point of death."

God has said: "If one member suffers, the whole body suffers with it."

God has said: "I am with you."

Then let's build together. So much work remains to be done.

More information concerning Brother Andrew's ministry, and the worldwide ministry of Open Doors, can be obtained from:

Open Doors, P.O. Box 6, Standlake, Witney, Oxon OX8 7SP.